"ISRAEL SERVED THE LORD"

Reading the Scriptures

Gary A. Anderson, Matthew Levering, and Robert Louis Wilken,
series editors

"ISRAEL SERVED THE LORD"

The Book of Joshua as Paradoxical Portrait of Faithful Israel

RACHEL M. BILLINGS

University of Notre Dame Press
Notre Dame, Indiana

Copyright © 2013 by University of Notre Dame
Notre Dame, Indiana 46556
www.undpress.nd.edu
All Rights Reserved

Published in the United States of America

Library of Congress Cataloging-in-Publication Data

Billings, Rachel M.
  "Israel served the Lord" : the Book of Joshua as paradoxical portrait of faithful Israel / Rachel M. Billings.
      pages   cm — (Reading the Scriptures)
  Includes bibliographical references and index.
  ISBN 978-0-268-02233-4 (pbk. : alk. paper) —
  ISBN 0-268-02233-X (pbk. : alk. paper)
  1. Bible. Joshua—Criticism, interpretation, etc.   I. Title.
  BS1295.52.B55   2013
  222'.206—dc23
                                    2013000462

∞ *The paper in this book meets the guidelines for permanence and durability of the Committee on Production Guidelines for Book Longevity of the Council on Library Resources.*

For Todd,

dedicated spouse and colleague

Contents

	Acknowledgments	ix
	Introduction: The Fragmentation of the Book of Joshua	1
ONE	"Israel Served the Lord": A Hermeneutical Key	11
TWO	The Stories of Rahab and Achan	25
THREE	The Gibeonites and the Transjordanian Altar	53
FOUR	The Extent of Israel's Occupation of the Land	95
	Conclusion: Israel *Did* Serve the Lord in the Book of Joshua	125
	Notes	133
	Bibliography	163
	Index	173

Acknowledgments

This book is based on my doctoral dissertation, which I successfully defended in March 2010; it was written in the Department of Near Eastern Languages and Civilizations in the Faculty of Arts and Sciences at Harvard University. Dissertations, although authored by a single person, inevitably emerge from a community. So many conversations and suggestions, advice and encouragement, influenced the shape of the completed work that it is impossible to provide an accounting of them all. Given that, here is an incomplete list of people to whom I owe thanks for their contributions: at Harvard, Dr. Jon D. Levenson, my principal adviser, and Dr. Gary Anderson and Dr. Paul Hanson, who rounded out my advising committee. Elsewhere, Dr. John Monson, who never fails to provide an encouraging word; all faculty friends who recalled how long it took them to finish their own dissertations; and the faculty of Western Theological Seminary, who always seemed to assume I would finish eventually. I must also give due credit to my colleagues, at Harvard and beyond, who formed the primary community within which my thoughts took shape: Karin Adams, Cory Crawford, Carrie Duncan, J. Randall Short, J. Todd Billings, Kyong-Jin Lee, Rachel Maxson, and so many others. In addition, I cannot neglect the biblical studies, archaeology, and ancient languages professors at Wheaton College (Illinois), especially Mr. Alfred Hoerth, who guided me through my undergraduate years, and the biblical studies faculty at the University of Notre Dame, who helped set me securely on my doctoral path. Finally, I give thanks to my family, whose faith and curiosity shaped me from my earliest days, and who encouraged me to pursue my educational aspirations, no matter how esoteric.

Introduction
The Fragmentation of the Book of Joshua

Two significant developments in biblical scholarship have converged to influence the reading of Joshua in the past century. First, a shift has occurred from the dominance of theories that more or less appended Joshua to source critical readings of the Pentateuch to the view that Joshua forms part of a larger Deuteronomistic History (DtrH). G. von Rad's classic essay "The Form-Critical Problem of the Hexateuch," published in 1938, exemplifies the former approach at its best.[1] In his reading, the book of Joshua served as closure for the story begun in the Pentateuchal books. Its origin in Solomon's nationalistic renaissance resulted in a focus on Israel's conquest of and claim to the land, and perhaps most importantly, on Israel *in* the land. This perspective soon fell by the wayside, though, when in 1943 Noth published his theory of the Deuteronomistic History, envisioning it as a brilliant, one-man project undertaken in exile. While other Deuteronomistic redactional theories preceded Noth,[2] the strength of his proposal lay in offering critical readers a momentary glimpse of a creatively composed whole: a persuasive synthesis that inspired a reconceptualization of the compositional history of the historical books of the Hebrew Bible. Although Noth's grand synthesis has been modified in many of its dimensions and even dismissed by some, it continues to reign supreme among critical scholars as the overarching framework for reading the books from Deuteronomy through Kings. With this development, then, the book of Joshua was swept up into a new context that shifted scholarly views of its relationship to the books before and after—not to mention the setting of its composition and ultimately the meaning of the stories it tells.

A second major development in twentieth-century biblical scholarship, which took place in the realm of trowels rather than texts, had bearing on scholarly readings of Joshua—that is, the floruit of the archaeology of the Levant. Even as Noth's theory came into print, archaeologists—Americans in particular—were attempting a grand synthesis of their own, wedding "dirt archaeology" with their explorations of the biblical text.[3] These discoveries would bring about another shift in scholarly readings of the historical books. As a result of these excavations, a new sort of data about the settlement of the land of Israel began to emerge, data based on reconstructed artifacts and occupation levels rather than texts. Confident dates and clear biblical parallels put forward by early enthusiasts were challenged as newer excavations reassessed the same evidence with better techniques—and different assumptions about how the Bible and the stuff in the dirt should be related to each other. Some archaeological readers of the Bible began to look to artifacts as the primary evidence by which to describe and explain the history of Israel. The clash between Garstang's and Kenyon's interpretations of the evidence at Jericho is iconic of this tension.[4] At the same time, it shows how far a reliance upon archaeological evidence had already made inroads into both archaeologically and textually focused assessments of the biblical stories. As a consequence of these discoveries and developments, nearly any scholar who reads and analyzes the biblical text relies upon a critical reconstruction of Israel's history whose evidential basis lies to some degree outside the text that he or she is reading, setting Israel's history per se at a distance from Israel's telling of it.

This book is written toward a concern that has been recognized and addressed by other scholars as well: that these historical excavations into both text and soil, concerned as they are with reconstruction, have neglected Israel's stories as a finished literary product, and have thereby missed some of what they say *as stories* rather than as sources of evidence. B. Child's distinction between "witness" and "source" summarizes this contrast from a theological angle: "To hear the text as witness involves identifying Israel's theological intention of bearing its testimony to a divine reality which has entered into time and space. Conversely to hear the text as source is to regard it as a vehicle of cultural expression which yields through critical analysis useful phenomenological data regarding Israel's societal life."[5] What Childs conveys in distinguishing between these two different approaches to the text is essentially two possible stances of the reader in relation to the text. When the reader approaches the text as "witness" or even as "storyteller," the reader's position is that of listener, hearing and entering into conversation with the text's story.[6] Conversely, when the reader approaches the text as "source," the reader's position is that of information-gatherer, with a concern for the usefulness of the text based on the reader's own purposes more than on a concern to hear the story the text has to tell.

This is true not only from the theological stance that Childs outlines above, but from a humanistic angle as well. Focusing on the utility of an object or entity can obscure our view of its beauty and artistry as a thing in itself. Certainly, for example, one can treat mountains as a source, mining them for ore, harvesting their lumber, and analyzing their geological origins. It would be a terrible mistake, however, to pursue these tasks so single-mindedly that one missed the majesty and awe-inspiring height of the mountains as features of the natural landscape. Moving to the realm of human craftsmanship, one could unravel a Persian carpet to examine its materials or to use the wool for some other purpose, or merely regard it as a handy floor-covering. To do so, however, would be to miss a central locus of the carpet's value and distinctiveness: namely, that it is a piece of human handiwork, intricately designed for beauty, and bearing beautiful decorative motifs developed within a long-standing tradition. Similarly, a text, too, can be broken down into its component parts to trace the origin of its content, or to access historical information it may contain. But we should be careful to balance this approach to the text as an informative historical relic with an appreciation of the text as an "artifact" in the truest sense of the word: a work of human artistry and ingenuity, whose value lies in its beauty as a created thing, not only in its usefulness.

The goal of this work, then, will be to address the past century's two great shifts in the reading of Joshua, looking at the text once again as a unitary entity and as itself an artifact worthy of study in its final form. The point of my reading will not be to determine the facts about how Israel came to be in the land of Canaan once and for all. Rather, the idea is to see how the shape of the story expresses the meaning of the book of Joshua as a written work. At the same time, my approach will take account of the fact that this book is a written work *from the past,* and thus that insights about its composition, style, and setting gleaned from modern scholarship can help us to become better readers of the story. In addition, I want to offer glimpses of the nature of this book as a written work *with* a past, and that insights into how to read it can be gained from other readers throughout the history of its reception.

Joshua as Part of the Deuteronomistic History

While investigations into the shape and editions of the Deuteronomistic History (DtrH) have frequently touched upon the book of Joshua, the book of Kings has often been chosen as a safer proving ground for such theories.[7] The apparently haphazard compilation of material in the book of Joshua—however artfully it may be arranged, literarily speaking—makes it challenging turf on which to stake one's claims regarding the date and manner of DtrH's composition. As a result, Joshua tends to get squeezed into the cracks left between readings of Deuteronomy and the royal history in Samuel-Kings. In addition, because the question of the date of DtrH's composition and redaction is intertwined with the kings of the late monarchy following Noth's initial proposal of an exilic work, the era of the kings inevitably receives more attention than Israel's earlier days under Joshua and the judges. Admittedly, the later books do provide more material to work with, simply by virtue of their greater length. In addition, more corroborative material from the broader ancient Near East is available from the Assyrian and Babylonian archives than exists for the purported span of Israel's early days in Canaan, so it offers more fruitful ground for cross-cultural comparison. In short, Joshua contains materials too varied in origin and relating to a period too early to make them ideal material for supporting stable theories of DtrH. Sandwiched between the imposing hulk of Deuteronomy and the protracted drama of the monarchy, Joshua tends to huddle together with Judges, sparring over claims to historical legitimacy.

For Noth, the material in Joshua did not, for the most part, derive directly from the pen of a Deuteronomistic historian (Dtr), but instead largely existed in a coherent sequence prior to the composition of the Deuteronomistic History. According to Noth, this "self-contained and detailed account, already existing in a fixed literary form" consisted of a string of etiological stories related to the conquest "combined into a well-rounded whole with a few heroic legends" before Dtr ever touched pen to scroll.[8] In most cases, the redactor only lightly retouched these stories to incorporate features of particular interest or concern to him, and modestly expanded upon this existing account.[9] Dtr's most significant independent contributions to the book are the introduction in chapter 1, which he composed entirely from scratch, and chapter 23, Joshua's closing oration, of a pattern common to the major speeches Dtr inserts periodically and judiciously throughout his history.[10]

Thus, while scholars often describe Noth's theory as attributing to the Deuteronomist the role of author, this does not most accurately describe his understanding of Dtr's role in the book of Joshua. Noth's reading of Joshua leaves a formidable amount of room for challenges to his single author–single edition theory, foreshadowing subsequent adaptations that will propose two or more editions of the Deuteronomist's work. According to his assessment, a later hand interpolated the material in chapters 13–21, supplementing DtrH's originally quite terse summation of the division of the land among the tribes in Joshua 11:23.[11] In addition, Joshua 24:1–28 also derives from a later hand—here, even Noth concedes, a Deuteronomistically influenced hand[12]—supplementing the original Deuteronomistic ending of Joshua's closing speech in chapter 23, which formerly was followed by the conclusion now shifted by this intervening material to chapter 24:29ff.

Noth understands the opening sequence of stories in Joshua 2–11 as etiological, drawing upon the work of H. Gressmann, who first suggested this analysis.[13] By *etiological,* he meant that these stories were back-formations, based on a present material reality or practice that the teller of the story sought to explain.[14] That is, these stories were composed to establish a cause-effect sequence, with the story of past causation written to make sense of a reality—the "effect"—contemporary with the storyteller. By this logic, the reality contemporary with the story's initiator is taken as a given, but the story itself tends to be understood as more or less derivative of that reality.

Indeed, the stories in the first half of the book of Joshua do not convey the impression of having been composed as a group, but rather culled from a traditional selection and assembled in a purposeful chain. Whether this sequencing is the work of the Deuteronomist or whether this chain preexisted his work remains open to question. The sequence of the stories suggests an awareness of their arrangement and overlap, so that although the stories themselves exhibit a remarkable variety of contents and formats, they intersect and mutually reflect upon one another. We shift abruptly from the naughty puns of the Rahab tale, to the somber Deuteronomic echoes of Achan's demise, to the blended trickster-treaty story of the Gibeonites. Explicit divine intervention in the conquest of Jericho gives way to divine silence regarding the fate of Gibeon. Yet the stories are bound together by recurring themes of interaction with clever foreigners, divine intervention in battle, cairns built over the graves of the wicked. Clearly they all share an association with Israel's earliest days inside the land, but apart from their present context, even that feature would be obscured. Instead, it seems that we are to look for the purpose of their assemblage in this particular context and sequence as the key to their meaning.

Many of these stories indeed involve some sort of persistent anchor that attaches it to a reality in Israel's present experience, thus suggesting the appropriateness of the "etiological" label. Whether the text points to inanimate markers such as the heaps of stones at the Jordan, Achan's mound, the ruins of Ai and the cairn over its king, or to the "living legends" of Rahab's family and the Gibeonites, these stories are peppered with reminders of Israel's earliest days in the land that exist "to this day."[15] Yet B. Childs rightly challenged both the clarity with which the etiological story had been defined and the implicit assumption that the explanatory story itself lay within the realm of myth and invention rather than within historical time. He argued that the label *etiological* would best be limited to stories of singular, reality-structuring events in mythic time that produced a lasting change that remained in effect in the present. Biblical stories of causation that account for specific historical realities should properly be distinguished from these mythic stories by some other designation, and their sequence of cause and effect should be open to examination from a historical, not only mythic, perspective. In addition, the function of these explanatory stories should be considered in relation to their context—literarily, theologically, and historically—rather than presumed to conform to a pre-established *religionsgeschichtliche* pattern.[16]

Along these lines, I would argue that these stories function not so much to explain the existence of the markers, as *the markers themselves exist*, but *to serve as touchstones for the stories as the biblical text presents them*, thus spurring Israel to see and to recall its origins in the land. Each of these ongoing realities serves as the stimulus or touchstone for a story about how YHWH brought Israel into its inheritance. To that degree, these stories are didactic in the best sense of the word; their value for Israel's instruction ranges from celebratory—recalling the miraculous crossing of the Jordan—to cautionary—underlining the dire consequences of violating YHWH's sacred command.

This common thread of "anchors" may suggest that the string of stories did in fact preexist its location in DtrH, rather than coming together as the product of Dtr's literary activity. Certainly stories connected with and reminding of Israel's entry into the land would have existed in advance of his composition of his own version of the history, and the lack of frequent and obvious literary intervention into these accounts in Dtr style suggests that the form of these stories as we have received them reflects their pre-Dtr form to some considerable degree. The fact that the sites associated with these early stories—namely, Jericho, Gilgal, Ai, and Gibeon—are clustered quite close together on the map bolsters the idea that a story complex existed in this area which Dtr adopted into his work. We might expect the stories to be preserved at Gilgal in particular if it was in fact the site of ongoing liturgical rituals associated with its sacred significance in the process of Israel's entry into the land. Thus, it seems entirely possible that the sequence of stories in the early chapters of Joshua stems from an earlier collection that Dtr incorporated into his work relatively intact.

Nonetheless, the sequence of stories in Joshua 2–11 exists not merely as an incorporated collection, but as an integral part of Dtr's account of Israel's settlement of the land as it stands. Presumably he could have selected variant traditions—perhaps even other complexes—which were in circulation; surely these were not the only stories told about Israel's earliest days. Yet this particular sequence reflects an interwoven dynamic of anticipation, fulfillment, and subversion, intertwining the three threads of YHWH, Israel, and the Canaanites in a complex network around the central theme of the land, which Dtr fully adopts as his own template for the book. The stories portray Israel's mixed history of obedience and disobedience, complete and incomplete reception of the land, and tension and harmony with other peoples which characterizes its present experience under Josiah as well.

Dtr establishes his ownership of these stories most clearly by splicing into them two key episodes that reflect his concern for the law. The first comes at the opening of the book, bracketing the entire story of Israel's occupation of the land within the theme of obedience as the key to success, firmly situating the law as Joshua's companion and guide in leading Israel, and interpreting military conquest as a task that remains wholly subject and subservient to the law rather than beside or outside of it (Josh 1:7-9). That is to say, the book of the Law is primary, and fearless facing of Israel's enemies in the land exists only as a subset of Israel's faithfulness to Torah. Israel's taking of the land is rooted once more in Mosaic obedience at the end of chapter 8, where Dtr ensures that the entire congregation hears the reading of the law and stands in the presence of the carved stones that record its words. Of course, the law stands outside of this sequence of stories, at the end of the book as well (Josh 23:6), recalling Israel once more to the basic principle of its existence, and reminding of its presence in Israel's midst. The Law is both faithful and inescapable in Israel's experience; Israel both receives its promised rewards and risks its threatened punishments by living in the presence of YHWH and His Law.

Recent Readings of Joshua

Literary and thematic studies written subsequent to the inception of the DtrH theory have demonstrated that the book of Joshua can continue to be read as a literary entity, presumably in the face of the facts (a) that it is a composite text and (b) that it is part of a larger work. In this book, I will interact primarily with five particular studies that have dealt with the book of Joshua as a literary unity to some degree. The significant studies that have dealt with Joshua in this way have covered a broad spectrum in their methods, focuses, and conclusions.[17]

A common theme among these readings of Joshua is one of the issues that will be of central interest to this work: namely, the tensions and themes that run throughout the length of the book. Robert Polzin, in *Moses and the Deuteronomist* (1980), understands these as competing "voices," with the more accommodating voice of "critical traditionalism" making itself heard over the stodgy voice of "authoritarian dogmatism" as regards the interpretation of the Law—a debate that begins in the book of Deuteronomy.[18] Nelson's article "Josiah in the Book of Joshua" (1981) is the most straightforwardly Deuteronomistic of the readings; Nelson interprets the figure of Joshua as a detailed prototype of Josiah. Briefly presented in his article "Joshua-Judges" in *The Literary Guide to the Bible* (1990), Gunn's perspective on the book's apparent contradictions is beautifully summarized in his conclusion, "In the gap between fulfillment and nonfulfillment we discover also the tension between divine justice and mercy."[19] Hawk, in *Every Promise Fulfilled* (1991), reads the book as an ominous interplay between two dominant strands: a portrait of complete fulfillment of all YHWH's promises to Israel, subverted by a dark undertow of Israel's failure and disobedience at every turn.[20] The result is that the assertions of fulfillment largely become empty truisms, while the reality is that Israel's actions mean that Israel's hopes are never fully consummated. Lastly, Mitchell's *Together in the Land* (1993) focuses on interactions and tensions between Israel and the nations in particular, arguing that the book projects a wistful ideal of a foreigner-free land while contending with the reality that Israel can never really be alone and autonomous.[21]

All of these literary-holistic studies, although they may vary in their level of persuasiveness and interest, have made valuable contributions to our reading of the book of Joshua. I do not seek to supplant what these other authors have written, but rather to supplement and build upon the readings that they have proposed.

ONE

"Israel Served the Lord"
A Hermeneutical Key

Above all, previous holistic readings of the book of Joshua have shown one thing: that any convincing reading must deal with the tensions that the book presents to the reader. Paradoxically, this multitude of tensions sends the reader in search of some theme or focal point by which to gather together the multifarious strands and weave them into an integrated story. That does not necessarily mean that the reader must find a way to eliminate the conflicting themes that pull at the fabric of the text. In fact, I suggest that the best reading will let these tensions remain as tensions, rather than try to eliminate them. Yet for the book to be read as a book, they must be rallied toward some common *telos*. That *telos*, I will argue, is the verdict in Joshua 24:31 that Israel "served the Lord during all the days of Joshua."[1] Many—perhaps most—scholars would read this verse as an exaggeration or an ironic declaration. I suggest instead that if the reader accepts this verse as a sincere statement, it becomes a literary clue pointing to a theological interpretation of the totality of Israel's actions in the book of Joshua. Specifically, it broadens and deepens the reader's understanding of Israel's service to the Lord, allowing it to encompass Israel's repentance and YHWH's mercy, not only Israel's obvious acts of obedience.

In four major narrative episodes in the book, Israel acts questionably in relation to YHWH's laws or commands.[2] These include the story of the oath to Rahab (Josh 2), Achan's violation of the ḥerem command (Josh 7), the treaty with the Gibeonites (Josh 9), and the altar built by the Transjordanian tribes (Josh 22). In addition, doubts remain in the book as a whole about whether Israel succeeds at the overall task of occupying the land, a task that also relates to Israel's obedience. This could lead the reader to take the statement of Israel's faithfulness in Joshua 24:31 as a hopeless contradiction or mere pious gloss. Instead, I will argue that it should be read as a "hermeneutical key" that simultaneously problematizes and illuminates these threads that have an ambiguous relationship to YHWH's prohibitions and commands.

At the conclusion of the book of Joshua, immediately preceding the burial notices of Joshua, the faithful "servant of the Lord,"[3] and Eleazar the priest, the text declares a sweeping verdict on the era of Joshua's leadership: "Israel served the Lord during all the days of Joshua and of all the elders who outlived him and who had experienced everything the Lord had done for Israel" (Josh 24:31). More than one commentator reads Joshua 24:31 as the stirring epitaph of one of Israel's great leaders, a tribute to his faithful example that kept the people on the right path during his lifetime and influenced the leadership of those who immediately followed him.[4] This conclusion would be perfectly logical, were it not that the contents of the book of Joshua call this verdict significantly into question. One might wonder whether the person who penned Joshua 24:31 actually read the book before inscribing such a positive conclusion, since Israel, as depicted in the book of Joshua, seems to have a rather mixed record of faithfulness in serving YHWH. Rather than drawing Israel's first days in the land as a steady line of obedient behavior and covenant faithfulness, the narrative vacillates between dramatic ups and downs, recounting the questionable alongside the upstanding.

It is true that the story begins with an extended and ceremonious entry into the land characterized by a harmonious call and response of command and action (Josh 3 and 4), followed by the long-neglected performance of circumcision (5:1–9) and the celebration of the Passover (5:10–12). With Israel's measured and graceful attentiveness to YHWH's instructions for the entry into the land and the references to removal of the "reproach of Egypt" (5:9) and the cessation of manna (5:12), the cumulative effect of the Jordan crossing is to mark the end of an era, and an auspicious new beginning for Israel: Israel, attentive to YHWH's commands, not rebellious; responsive, not resisting; tasting the firstfruits of the fulfillment of all YHWH's promises in the long-promised land (5:12).

But not all of Israel's actions in the book are characterized by the moving *gravitas* and *pietas* that envelop these first moments and days of newness and promise. By the time we reach the positive assessment of Israel's behavior at the end of the book, an oath has been made to a Canaanite prostitute and her household, exempting them from the *ḥerem* decree, and the Gibeonites have tricked their way into a treaty that accomplishes the same. Both actions seem highly questionable in light of Deuteronomic legislation regarding Israel's relationship to inhabitants of the land.[5] Perhaps worse yet, Achan—an Israelite!—has violated the *ḥerem* decree himself by pilfering choice items from the devoted goods of Jericho, an action that temporarily places an unwitting Israel under the ban. Finally, after the allotment of the land, when at last it appears that rest will follow, the Reubenites, the Gadites, and half-Manasseh construct a conspicuous altar of doubtful legitimacy and purpose as they return to their portion across the river, throwing all Israel into turmoil once more. In addition to these incidents related more extensively in narrative, the description of the division of the land is peppered with mentions of the land's previous inhabitants still remaining in Israelite territory and notes on land not yet taken,[6] calling into question both Israel's application of the *ḥerem* command and its faithfulness in occupying the land. Even Joshua's concluding exhortations cast new doubt on Israel's behavior, since his urging that the people "throw away the gods that you worshiped beyond the River and in Egypt" (24:14) implies—for the first time in the book—that Israel's allegiance may not in fact be exclusively to YHWH.

In light of all of these dubious actions, it seems that the summarizing conclusion in Joshua 24:31 is more surprising and problematic than rousing. Historical critics know immediately where to place the blame: presumably upon one of the Deuteronomists, based on the statement's retrospective air; concern for the periodization of Israel's history;[7] and lack of natural and readily apparent coherence with the book it is attached to. Whether the redactor is figuratively blind, overly optimistic, or merely stupid, his tidy statement threatens to flatten—or at very least contradict—the complicated course of events that has led up to this moment in the process of Israel's occupation of Canaan within the book of Joshua. On the face of it, this statement reads more like a gloss that attempts to level distinctions and erase divergences, oblivious to the complexities of Israel's actions, than like a logical conclusion regarding Israel's covenant faithfulness under Joshua.

Perhaps what is most surprising about previous scholars' readings of Joshua 24:31 is how many seem to be unbothered by it. More commentators than one would expect read this verse exactly at face value, taking it completely in stride, as if nothing in the book of Joshua had suggested that Israel at any point significantly failed to serve YHWH under Joshua's leadership. It is unclear what motivates this lack of attention to the verse in most cases. Some commentators fail to see any tension between this verse and the events that precede it in the book of Joshua, though the reader must wonder how much this perspective ignores the textual evidence for such tension. Some part of the blame should also lie on two opposite tendencies of commentaries, each of which has its weaknesses in the treatment of "glosses" such as this one. One variety takes a piecemeal approach to the text, moving through the text verse by verse, attending closely to the technical details of each verse, but as a result often neglecting or dodging the question of what the verses might actually mean in relation to each other. Another sort divides the text into titled or themed blocks, which it then proceeds to interpret;[8] this approach, however, can miss the trees for the forest in its concern to demarcate tidy units rather than dealing with the messiness of the minutiae.

Commentators who do notice the verse tend to take it, quite logically, as a turning point between the generation under Joshua and the period of the judges.[9] Not only does it perform this function by defining the era of Joshua in a certain way, but its nearly verbatim correspondence to Judges 2:7, similarly set alongside a report of Joshua's death, points to the "hinge" function of this verse.[10] The context of each verse conveys the distinction between the two eras even more sharply. In Joshua, it follows the covenant ceremony of chapter 24, which concludes with Israel's bold ostensible choice of YHWH against Joshua's warning of the impossibility of the task, a harbinger of what is to come. In Judges, the verse accompanies a notice of Israel's failure, as predicted, to serve the Lord faithfully, deepening the rift between the era of Joshua and the cycle of disobedience that ensues under the judges. As such, it is broadly understood as a literary device—presumably deployed by a Deuteronomistic compiler-redactor—that links the two books and defines their relationship to each other. Its nearly verbatim correspondence to Judges 2:7, also linked with a report of Joshua's death, indicates this connection.

From a related but slightly different angle, it is often viewed as a characteristic or definitive statement regarding Israel under Joshua,[11] as its sweeping nature and its location at the close of the book, following the dramatic moment of decision to serve YHWH, might suggest. Commentators who focus on this dimension of its function describe it in ways that recognize it as a point of culmination, whether the climax of the theme of serving the Lord, noting its use of the verb *ᵓbd* which has been reiterated multiple times in chapter 24,[12] or as a positive note of covenant fidelity on which the whole story of Joshua's leadership ends.[13] While these two understandings of the statement seem mutually compatible, capturing different dimensions of the statement's function as a literary device, they do little to explain its function in relation to the contents of the book that seem to diverge from this sunny picture of the era of Joshua. Can we really read this statement as "ringing testimony to Israel's loyalty to the covenant," as one commentator effusively frames it?[14] It seems that our assertion regarding the parity of redactional assertions with other dimensions of the text must here meet its counterpart, the assertion that the contents of the text must be allowed full voice in relation to redactional assertions. To do full and equal justice to both this statement and the rest of the book of Joshua requires us to offer further explication of the statement beyond its immediate context and beyond a shallow acceptance of what it says.

Joshua 24:31 and Israel's Unfaithful Actions in the Book

It seems to me that a proper understanding of this "verdict" takes it neither as an ideological imposition on the text, threatening to eliminate the mixed portrait of Israel's actions in the book of Joshua in favor of a neat scheme of either-or, heads-or-tails history, nor as the calculated work of a redactor who wanted to create an artificial contrast with the era of the judges. In my opinion, both of these evaluations fail by refusing to take the statement in Joshua 24:31 as an integral part of the text that we now call the book of Joshua. Historically speaking, the verdict certainly comes later in the text's history than the earliest rituals, stories, or lists that eventually came to be part of this work. But although it is apparently the work of a redactor who postdates much of the composition of the book's materials, it has now been incorporated into the fabric of the book—a fabric whose texture and patterns have themselves been shaped by the hand of a redactor. A reading whose primary goal is to respect and encounter the book of Joshua's identity and integrity as text sees this statement as "belonging" to the book just as much as any of its other materials. Such a reading puts this statement on equal footing with content that does not originate with the redactor rather than singling it out for scrutiny based on a historical hierarchy of textual preference. When the text is read as a temporally simultaneous literary work, oldest is not best; all is text. The constituent parts "compete" for importance on the basis of their literary function or prominence rather than on the basis of their antiquity.

Conventional labels such as "gloss" or "redactional addition" fail to capture the function of this statement, alienating the content in question too much from the text in which it occurs. For the purposes of my reading, I will functionally replace them with the phrase *hermeneutical key*, intentionally directing attention to the statement's role as an interpretive device in relation to the contents of the book.[15] Read as such, this "key"—and others like it—calls the reader to evaluate what has come before, perhaps in a surprising new light. Herein we find the function and purpose of this particular statement, most probably introduced by a redactor. What this "hermeneutical key" unlocks, I will argue, is a notion that can give hope to readers who fear that their failure to serve the Lord faithfully will be their doom. By the strictest application of justice, there should *be* no Israel by the close of the book. Instead, the juxtaposition of this statement with the difficult stories of Israel's ambiguous or unfaithful actions in the text shows that where obedience fails, repentance can fill the gap between good intentions and divine justice.[16] The directness and unequivocality of the surprising verdict at the book's conclusion, in spite of all that has occurred between auspicious start and foreboding finish, awaken the reader to the mercy that has been divinely given in the course of the book. Its position in the final chapter of the book ensures that no action of Israel's will slip under the wire and escape this "blanket" of mercy, while at the same ominously announcing that the era of Joshua's successful guidance of Israel is about to come to an end.[17]

Part of the reason that hermeneutical statements like the one in Joshua 24:31 can work is that they do not work alone; they are the tips of icebergs that consist of the overall arrangement and structure of the text. These statements serve to manifest in compact form the meaning of the larger patterns that undergird and are at work in the text. While the contents of the book of Joshua may derive from diverse sources and traditions, their present inclusion is hardly accidental. Although the text may interrupt itself, so to speak, or even contend with itself, these points of tension serve to indicate that broader, subtler patterns are present. The particular usefulness of such blunt assessments as the one offered in chapter 24 is that they bring these tensions to a head, pulling to the surface of the text what has previously been visible only as threads woven through it.[18] Such statements offer a degree of clarity by their forthrightness, yet they also inevitably call attention to discrepancies between their own claims and counterclaims within the broader text by their very assertion of those claims. In so doing, they enable the text, its redactors, and readers to tolerate the tensions within it, by implicitly acknowledging those tensions and harnessing them in a meaningful way—providing a rubric for reading, a means *within* the text of "making sense" of its divergent parts.[19] Because they provide an entry point into the meaning of the diverse contents of Joshua, they actually *permit* the tensions to exist in the book rather than subjecting them to a *ḥerem* of their own.[20]

Certainly the idea of the provision of such a key within the text can have a didactic ring to it, with all the subtlety of the "moral" bluntly tacked on to the end of an Aesop's fable—a conclusion that, for many readers today, would effectively ruin a good story. In this case, however, I would argue that this statement harnesses the ambiguity of the text for the purposes of moral evaluation only to turn it into surprise. It requires readers to take a second look at their expectations and at the events that have taken place in the book, to realize that everything may not have been as it seemed—that far more violations have been committed and far more mercy has been given than the reader may at first have realized. In so doing, it displays a Deuteronomistic concept of Law-keeping that goes beyond the caricature too often assumed: that the Deuteronomic Law has room only for automatic reward and punishment, blessing and curse seamlessly matched to obedience and disobedience. Instead, it presents a portrait that includes the possibility of violation and restoration, which resonates with Deuteronomy's overall tone of hope for repentance.

I would argue, then, that this statement should be taken seriously as a theological interpretation of the contents of the book as they relate to Israel's faithful service of YHWH. This may seem simplistic enough, and perhaps too similar to the purposes of the aforementioned ideologically driven or clumsy redactor. I mean more, however, by saying the statement should be taken seriously than simply that it is "right," and that we should all agree with the redactor's evaluation of things and move on. Rather, I am arguing that reading redactional statements in a way that reckons them to be an organic part of the texts in which they occur actually brings their purpose in the text to the fore. When these statements are read as part of the book rather than surface features, the contradictions and tensions in the story become more than mere accidents of redaction; rather, they can be seen as an integral and substantial part of the book.[21] Taken in this way, these statements have now become *hermeneutical clues* that unlock the story and its meaning rather than impositions of an external perspective upon it. It becomes the reader's task to determine how it is that all of the things that occur in or are spoken in the course of the story can be true at once. The simultaneity of the text's many perspectives and contributions becomes part of a puzzle rather than a collection of disconnected fragments, or competitors for a limited turf of "rightness."

What becomes most prominent in this text-as-text reading, to summarize the point, is *function* rather than age, in discerning how an individual statement relates to the rest of the book. I will argue in this chapter that the verdict that "Israel served the Lord during all the days of Joshua" does not merely sweep all of Israel's actions preceding it under the rug of editorial license and propriety. Comparison with the book of Deuteronomy, on the one hand, and evaluations of Israel's behavior within the book of Joshua, on the other, make it impossible for Israel's "service" to be interpreted as simplistically faithful by any standards available to the reader, either within the text of Joshua or in canonical works that seem to have been shaped by a Deuteronomistic hand. Rather than simplifying the reader's comprehension of the book's contents—that is, *reducing* all of Israel's actions to piety and goodwill—this statement, I argue, works in the *opposite* way: it radically complexifies the notion of faithful service of the Lord. Rather than eliminating anything inconsistent with this verdict, the inclusion of this statement turns the tables and challenges the reader's understanding of obedience as either flawless or useless. By this verdict, all of Israel's actions in the book of Joshua—both failures and successes—are bound together and wrapped up in a covering of mercy that allows repentance to "count" for faithful service of YHWH.

Deuteronomic Law in Relation to the Book of Joshua

Since much of the tension in these stories arises from the degree to which Israel keeps or fails to keep the laws and commands of Deuteronomy, it seems relevant to offer an overview of the function of the book of the Law within Joshua as the proper background against which to examine these particular stories. Even though the book of Joshua contains only a few mentions of the book of the Law, Robert Polzin was on the right track when he described Israel as "occupying the law" as well as the land in Joshua.[22] Like the book of Psalms, Joshua opens with a strikingly direct focus on the Law that seems situated to serve as a preface and focal point for reading. The compiler or redactor draws our attention to a point that might not otherwise be foremost in readers' minds as they embark upon their exploration of the ritual actions, battle accounts, and land divisions that follow.

In spite of the book of Joshua's reputation for violent mandates, massive slaughter, and stories of military conquest, the Lord's initial commissioning of Joshua at the outset of the book has little to say about any of these things and much to say about the Law. Readers often associate the Lord's threefold admonition to "be strong and courageous"[23] in this opening scene with the stalwart and fearless leadership Joshua will have to display in order to lead his troops successfully in battle. In the context of the first chapter of Joshua, however, these commands have only partly to do with courage in battle. Although they certainly relate to the taking of the land at this level of military involvement, they are interwoven with the necessity of keeping the Law and the Lord's commands if Israel is to succeed in receiving its inheritance by any means. What the Lord is most concerned to enjoin upon this new leader of his people is a courageous keeping of the Law. Obedience, not merely battle-worthiness, is at stake.[24]

Like Psalm 1, this chapter sets the tone for the rest of the book that it prefaces, offering the reader clues as to what will be important in the ensuing chapters and narratives. It frames the book in such a way that the "plot" seeks not only to answer the more obvious question "Will Israel succeed in taking possession of the land?" but to compound it by asking, "Will Israel *keep the law and thereby* succeed in taking possession of the land?" In the way that the answer to this question develops, it becomes clear that yet another question is contained within these questions and is very much at stake, namely, "Will Israel succeed in being Israel?" This question embraces both of the others within its scope, since Israel's inheritance of the land is consequent upon its identity as Israel, the chosen people of YHWH. Israel's identity as Israel is constituted by its place as party to YHWH's covenant and recipient of YHWH's law, such that Israel's identity as Israel cannot exist apart from its attachment to the Law, such that Israel cannot in fact benefit from YHWH's promises, including inheritance of the land, apart from its *obedience* to the Law. Thus, Israel's success in the book of Joshua becomes defined in terms that go far beyond mere military conquest. Success in this area will instead appear as a result of broader patterns in Israel's behavior vis-à-vis YHWH, His covenant, and His commands: land, identity, and obedience are inseparably intertwined.

Few explicit references to a written law book exist in the book of Joshua, though these few firmly anchor the theme in the book's fabric. All five mentions of the book of the Torah occur in sections that are among the book's more expressly theological material, and clearly derive from a Deuteronomistic hand. The first of these is found in the opening chapter, which recounts Joshua's commissioning ("Do not let this book of the law depart from your mouth," 1:8) and highlights the centrality of law and obedience in the book. Two others are found in the covenant ceremony in chapter 8 (v. 31 and v. 34), and the final two occur in the covenant ceremony at the end of the book (23:6, 24:26).

This first occurrence, positioned so early in the book of Joshua, has a programmatic character, calling the reader's attention to specific (yet unspecified) written material present and available at the time when the Lord speaks to Joshua across the Jordan. Remarkably—no less so because it is common for Dtr—it situates the written word of the Lord as guide alongside the presently spoken word of the Lord. These two forms of divine speech are not distinguished as markers of different eras in Israel's history; rather, they are available and to be drawn upon simultaneously. At other points in the book, the simultaneity of these two media of divine communication is reinforced by the presence of direct divine speech at some points and its absence at others.[25] Like the sun, sometimes hidden by cloud and sometimes blazing in its full radiance, YHWH sometimes makes Himself radically present in Joshua, and at other times is conspicuous by His absence. As a result, reliance upon the written word is implicit, even though the Law book's presence is made known to the reader primarily through the exhortations in chapter 1, with reminders positioned judiciously at other points in the book.[26] But while this written law is in Joshua's hands, immediately present in the midst of the people, it requires the mediation of reading and interpretation to serve as their guide. Thus, as Polzin has previously observed, this undertaking upon which the Israelites are about to embark will involve an interpretation of this law coterminous with the occupation of the land.[27] Both contain terrain/territory that has yet to be explored and inhabited, as Israel becomes a settled people for the first time.

By positioning the book of the Law prominently and judiciously at key moments in the narrative, the redactor of the Joshua materials seems to be prodding the reader to consider Israel's actions under Joshua in relation to YHWH's commands, whether in their written form or in YHWH's present address. On the one hand, in some cases Israel's departure from YHWH's word is readily apparent, as in the matter of Achan's violation of the *ḥerem* and of the treaty with the Gibeonites. On the other hand, the stories of Rahab and of the Transjordanian altar do not bear such a clear relationship to the Lord's previous commands, but nonetheless beg for evaluation. The oath made to Rahab by the spies in chapter 2 is neither directly condemned nor undeniably portrayed as a violation, but needs to be related to the Deuteronomic commands to subject all Canaanites to the *ḥerem*. Similarly, the incident involving the altar built by the Transjordanians in Joshua 22 seems to take as its touchstones Deuteronomic norms regarding central sacrifice and Deuteronomy's prescribed response to inner-Israelite apostasy. Yet it concludes by approving a noncentralized altar in a way that places it in an uncertain relationship to the Law.[28] Finally, Israel's failure to eradicate the Canaanites as commanded in Deuteronomy and its need for injunctions to finish occupying the land point to further questions about the extent of Israel's obedience to YHWH.

The question of the relationship between Israel's actions in the book of Joshua and YHWH's written and immediate commands takes on crucial implications for our understanding of Dtr's portrayal of Israel under Joshua's leadership. Given its record of actions under Joshua, has Israel obeyed or violated the Law? Is Joshua's Israel an ideal for future generations, or is it already entering the early stages of its decay and failure vis-à-vis the covenant? As a story to be told to future generations, does this segment of the history of Israel serve as a model or as a warning? Joshua 24:31 renders the decisive verdict, but only a closer look at the problematic stories themselves can show how Israel's faithfulness under Joshua is ultimately affirmed.

How Did Israel Serve the Lord?

In arguing for this conclusion, this work will explore four major stories and a central theme in the book of Joshua that seem to challenge—or even falsify—the statement that "Israel served the Lord" under Joshua's leadership. These stories include the account of the spies' encounter with Rahab, Achan's violation of the *ḥerem*, the Gibeonites' treaty-making deception, and the altar built by the Transjordanians; alongside these stands the question of the extent of Israel's occupation of the land which is raised by the book's uneven treatment of the issue. What distinguishes these particular stories and this theme is their prominence in the book combined with the fact that each contains an action that may range from questionable to clearly violating the Lord's command, with the latter posing a particular challenge to the statement that "Israel served the Lord." Textually speaking, these are the points at which the greatest tension is generated between the book of Joshua and its literary and canonical context within the broader DtrH.[29]

Using the statement of Joshua 24:31 as a hermeneutical key to "unlock" these sections of the text draws out a dilemma related to Israel's faithfulness that each of them poses. I will examine these texts in light of the conclusion that Israel served the Lord under Joshua, using this statement as a "key" to unlock the meaning and purpose of each of these texts within the book. In so doing, I will demonstrate that each incident of Israel's questionable or disobedient action in these stories is resolved in a way that allows Israel to continue to exist before YHWH and stand within His favor. Reading the stories in this light yields, in turn, hermeneutical clues for future Israelites who are the story's readers, seeking instruction from this first, foundational generation in the land regarding what it means to be faithful to YHWH and His Law in a way that enables Israel to remain in the land. The cumulative effect of these stories is ultimately to convey that Israel's faithfulness in the book of Joshua is found not only in the people's straightforward acts of obedience, of which there are certainly many, but in Israel's efforts to act according to the Law in unexpected and unfamiliar situations, and in YHWH's generous mercy making room for the times when they fail.

TWO

The Stories of Rahab and Achan

The stories of Rahab and Achan will serve as the first locus of our investigation into the tensions in the book of Joshua and the purpose that these tensions serve within the narrative. I have grouped these two stories together because of the way in which they can be seen to function as mirror images of each other, as a number of scholars have observed.[1] In the first, the character of Rahab offers a surprising contrast with the dire warnings against Canaanites as representatives of idolatry in the book of Deuteronomy. Contrary to Dtr's basic portrayal of the Canaanites as a threat, Rahab serves as the agent of YHWH's deliverance of the spies, confirming YHWH's promises to Israel by her dramatic break with our expectations about the function of Canaanites in the story of Israel's settlement. This spurs us to further investigate the narrative role of her character and the purpose of this subversion of expectations.

The second story, recounting Achan's theft of goods placed under the *ḥerem*, provides a grim rather than triumphant glimpse into Israel's early days in the land. In contrast to the wonder of YHWH's unexpected mercy through the fidelity of a Canaanite, we encounter the careless and unthinking infidelity that Achan's lust for plunder inspires. At the same time, the story offers a meditation on the methods and presuppositions of the ensuing divine justice that is enacted in Israel's midst, turning treason into a reminder of Israel's appropriate response to divine wrath, and turning Israel toward the perennial possibility—and responsibility—of repentance. As a pair, the stories demonstrate for Israel the possibility of fidelity without and treachery within, warning against deceptive appearances while schooling Israel in the art of seeking out and identifying YHWH's often surprising work on its behalf.

Illicit Oath or Covenant Ally? The Paradox of Rahab the Canaanite

With its cast of a prostitute and two spies who use deception and a questionable oath to achieve their respective ends, the story of Rahab in Joshua 2 has proved both fascinating and bothersome to interpreters. As Jerome Creach so enthusiastically phrases it, "The narrative has suspense, sexual innuendo, and an underdog who triumphs—everything a modern audience expects in a great story!"[2] Yet these same features that make the account in Joshua 2 a "great story" in modern eyes have also presented some exegetical challenges. The tale presents us with two potentially significant problems: first, the role of Rahab in the story—namely, how does the forthright identification of Israel's deliverer as a Canaanite prostitute function in the account; and second, the possible violation of Deuteronomic law by the oath the spies make to her—specifically, does the oath conflict with the prohibitions on making covenants with or showing mercy to Canaanites set forth in Deuteronomy 7? With regard to the first tension, I will argue that Rahab's identification as a Canaanite and a prostitute functions primarily to highlight YHWH's surprising acts on behalf of Israel, provoking the spies' exclamation, after they have reported their narrow escape, that "YHWH has surely given the land into our hands!" (Josh 2:24). In dealing with the second tension, I will propose that the oath made by the spies in fact "fits into the gaps" of the Law rather than violating it, demonstrating an exception to the *ḥerem* for a YHWH-honoring Canaanite who allies herself with Israel. In short, Israel's choices and actions in this chapter, though they may be unexpected, are not unfaithful—and YHWH acts within the story by equally improbable means.

Previous Readings of Rahab

Ironically, but perhaps unsurprisingly, early Jewish and Christian interpreters found fewer problems with this text than have modern historical-critical readers. Because these early interpreters read the story within the broader framework of creative inner-scriptural exegesis and assumptions about the unity of Scripture, with an eye for the story's application to the life of contemporary religious communities, they had more tools and objectives at their disposal for making sense of it. Premodern interpreters, as it turns out, gave the majority of their attention to the figure of Rahab. A few early Christian readers wrestled with the ethical consequences of the lie she uses to protect the spies, but most ultimately praised her as an example of radical repentance, a model of hospitality, or a type of the church.[3] Some rabbinic readers quibbled with her profession,[4] but others wed her to Joshua and incorporated her into Israelite lineages;[5] more frequently, she took her place in lists of righteous Gentiles, alongside Jethro and Ruth.[6]

Historical-critical readers, on the other hand, having little recourse to notions of figural meaning, the unity of Scripture, or practical application, have had more difficulty in choosing the most suitable framework for interpreting the story. Some readers have focused their attention on how the story of Rahab fits into one or more of a number of classic folkloric story types; readings of this sort often emphasize her character as a crafty prostitute who exploits her advantage in the situation to get what she wants from the spies.[7] Others, often under the same guise, make much of the sexual double entendres in the story. Whatever linguistic or historical attempts might be made to sanitize Rahab's profession as that of "innkeeper" or "barmaid,"[8] it is true that sexual innuendos and naughty puns can easily be found throughout the story by those who seek them.⁹ Yet those who would place the emphasis on coarse humor would miss the story's purpose in its present context, which raises significant challenges to this line of interpretation. Despite its colorful telling, the remarkable story of Rahab takes on a broader role in relation to the narrative of Israel's occupation of the land, as Dtr has shaped it to lead us toward awe of YHWH's unlikely acts of deliverance on behalf of Israel rather than to titillate us with the stuff of bawdy folklore.

This point aside, historical-critical readers' concerns about the ethical dimensions of the narrative for the most part lie elsewhere than with Rahab. Interestingly, critical scholars express more distress about the potential conflict between the oath that the spies make to Rahab and Deuteronomic law than did early Jewish and Christian readers. Commentators who discuss this oath generally regard it as at best standing in tension with, and at worst blatantly violating, the limits imposed by Deuteronomic commands forbidding Israel to show mercy to or make covenants with the Canaanite population of the land.[10] Given the seriousness of this accusation, it seems strange that few give this supposed violation much attention beyond merely observing its presence.[11] Rather, it seems implicitly to be relegated to the realm of literary contradictions, which for historical-critical readers often serve as little more than red flags signaling disparate sources. Another possible explanation of why it is so easily forgotten is the lack of a punitive divine response following the oath. We see this as reflected in the fact that unlike Achan's clear-cut and obvious portrayal as a violator of the covenant, historical-critical readers are more likely to see the spies as merely slipshod or bumbling rather than as flagrant offenders.

Only L. D. Hawk goes on to explore in detail how potentially grave this misdeed might really be, if it indeed is reckoned as a covenant violation. For Hawk, Rahab is an ominous figure who uses the spies' awkward situation to her advantage and leads them into outright transgression of the covenant.[12] As he explains, "Rahab personifies the temptation to apostatize" as woman, Canaanite, and prostitute.[13] As the counterparts of this looming Canaanite figure, he sees the spies as weak-willed and wobbly-kneed, such that "they are willing, without hesitation, to abandon obedience to YHWH's commandments for the sake of an expedient resolution to their predicament."[14] In short, "the spies opt for survival over obedience"[15] in acceding to Rahab's demand.

How, then, do we relate to Deuteronomic law what transpires between Rahab and the spies? Does Israel indeed act disobediently by granting Rahab her life? To answer these questions, we first must answer how Rahab as a character fits into the story. Is the Canaanite prostitute inherently a figure who bodes ill for Israel, or little more than a narrative device? Does the text portray her as an earnest ally, wholeheartedly on the side of Israel, or as a manipulative shrew, interested only in preserving her own life? Second, we must examine the legality of the oath the spies make to Rahab in light of Deuteronomic laws governing Israel's relationship with the Canaanites, particularly the *ḥerem* commands in chapters 7 and 20. Does the spies' oath indeed violate these commands, or can Rahab be considered a legitimate exception? To answer these two sets of questions is to shed light on the answers to both, and thus gain a better understanding of the function of this story and its tensions within the book of Joshua and DtrH as a whole. We will see that this story offers an extension rather than a violation of the Deuteronomic laws—filling a gap with regard to a situation that the law does not address—and ultimately pointing to YHWH's mercy toward Israel in His surprising choice of deliverer.

The Role of Rahab

Speculations about the spies' purposes in entering a house in the "red light district" of Jericho are largely beside the point, mainly giving some commentators the opportunity to label others as prudes. Although prostitution would eventually become a powerful metaphor for Israel's straying from YHWH to the Baals, common prostitution was not actually forbidden in ancient Israel.[16] As a result, any nonverbal exchanges between the spies and this woman in her professional capacity are actually inconsequential to the story. This is not, however, to agree with Soggin that "the role which this woman plays [in the narrative] has nothing to do with her profession."[17] Quite the contrary, it matters a great deal in three ways: first, it is instrumental to the plot, in that Rahab's profession gives the spies either a reason (or a pretense) for lodging at Rahab's house during their reconnaissance mission; second, it tells us something about the social location of Rahab as a character, since prostitution develops a distinctly negative connotation in Israel in spite of its apparent legality; and third, it emphasizes YHWH's agency in delivering the spies by providing rescue from such an unexpected quarter.

Whether it is love or lodging that the spies seek, the house of a prostitute is a particularly suitable choice for men who do not wish to answer questions about their purposes in the city. Even so, they hardly expect the welcome from the house's proprietress that they receive. Early interpreters, rather than questioning the spies' motives in entering Rahab's house, drew attention instead to Rahab's graciousness to these strangers. No matter what their purposes may have been, Rahab demonstrates hospitality in sheltering them from the king's men, and this kindness earns her a reputation for hospitality in early Christian writings parallel to that of Lot, who shelters the two messengers from the inhabitants of Sodom in Genesis 19. Even those interpreters who are wary of Rahab's lie see her mercy in hiding the Israelite spies as so great that she receives full forgiveness for the falsehood she tells in the course of successfully accomplishing their concealment.

Yet although Rahab's profession makes her house a strategic choice for the spies, it inevitably locates her on the margins of society to some degree. Though a Talmudic source suggests that Rahab was a courtesan of high status, sought out by rulers far and wide[18]—similar to F. M. Cross's more recently expressed opinion that she was well known as a figure of legend[19]—her profession dooms her to a common fate, however famous she may be as a result of it. As a woman without a husband or hope of producing heirs, she lacks any means of fulfilling the role for which women were normally most valued in ancient Near Eastern societies; even if she is honored, she is an anomaly. Furthermore, while common prostitution is never outlawed in ancient Israel, the texts that we possess indicate that it is the resort of those in financial need, and not a reputable profession for a woman. Prostitutes may not use their earnings in payment of vows (Deut 23:18), perhaps deterring people from turning to prostitution in order to fulfill a religious financial commitment they have made.[20] Fathers are forbidden by a law in Leviticus to make their daughters available as prostitutes, presumably for financial exploitation (Lev 19:29); Gottwald, in fact, suggests an economic motivation for Rahab's employment, noting that "the fact that [Rahab] is represented as living with her father's *beth-av* may mean that she was pushed into harlotry to support her family."[21]

Narrative examples of the negative associations of prostitution reinforce these legal ones. Dinah's brothers in Genesis 34:21 rely upon the stigma of prostitution in their challenge to their father regarding Shechem's action: "Should he treat our sister as a prostitute?" Because Jephthah was mothered by a prostitute, his brothers expel him from the household and disinherit him, seizing upon his birth by another woman as a cause for alienation (Jdg 11:1–2). Finally, Tamar in Genesis 38, while ultimately reckoned as a heroine and justified in her deed, uses deception and subterfuge to trick her father-in-law into impregnating her through prostitution. Judah's subsequent call for her to be burned upon discovery of her pregnancy may well turn upon the classification of her prostitution as adultery, since she was technically betrothed to his youngest son. Even so, we can point to the lingering air of embarrassment around the fact that when Judah sends his payment and the prostitute is nowhere to be found, he quickly calls off the search, despite the fact that she still possesses some very personal mementos belonging to him (Gen 38:18, 23). Again, there seems to be no condemnation for his consorting with a prostitute, yet at the same time, the story presents his tryst as a sensitive and rather private matter that he does not wish to advertise. Tamar, like Rahab, is ultimately justified as the heroine of the story, despite initial appearances.

Based on these examples, we can conclude that the material dealing with the notion and practice of common prostitution in ancient Israel points to negative associations surrounding the practice, even though it appears to be tolerated. Thus, Rahab's identification primarily as a prostitute should raise in readers a degree of wariness regarding what will ensue, followed by her ultimate vindication as a true—though unexpected—friend of Israel.

Rahab's Confession

The story quickly dispels any premonitions that may have been raised by the spies' initial entry into the house of a Canaanite prostitute, as it launches almost immediately into an account of Rahab's actions on behalf of the spies. By the time the king's searchers come around, she has already hidden the visiting Israelites on her roof (Josh 2:4–6). Her claim that the men have left the building and that she never knew where they came from in the first place (2:4) humorously contrasts with the detailed testimony she presents to the spies regarding the history of Israel's movements and purposes once the kings' messengers are out of the way.[22] Rahab's speech and actions reveal that this first Canaanite whom the Israelites encounter in the land does not fit the image that Deuteronomy 7 presents of the inhabitants that are to be committed to ḥerem. She does not even express solidarity with her people by turning the spies over to the authorities, much less compel these Israelites to bow down to her idols to secure her help. Instead, she confesses YHWH, as her actions have already done.[23] She reports on His deeds eloquently and at length, and concludes by recounting the terror that has befallen her own people at the report of what He has done for Israel (2:8–9, 11). Rather than challenging or threatening Israel's possession of the land, she confirms it and aids in it.

Furthermore, within her confession is embedded a statement about YHWH with yet more significance. Joshua 2:11 employs the phrase "in heaven above and on earth below," a rare but significant combination that occurs in only three passages within DtrH (Deut 4:29, Josh 2:11, 1 Kgs 8:23) and once outside of it (Eccl 5:6), as N. MacDonald has observed.[24] To explicate the phrase, he begins with the antithetical use of the pair in Ecclesiastes to establish a contrast between the location of the divine ("in heaven above") and the human ("on earth below"). He supports his understanding of this usage with other passages that speak only of YHWH dwelling in heaven, without the attendant contrast with humankind. Because these passages deal with the particular matter of YHWH's location, he concludes that the phrase, as used in Deuteronomy 4:29, "makes a statement about YHWH's *presence,* not about the extent of his power" (emphasis mine).[25] This statement, in turn, he grounds in the preceding account in Deuteronomy 4:15ff of the Horeb theophany "in the voice and fire,"[26] which undergirds Israel's confession of YHWH's unique and aniconic presence with His people, and Israel's consequent shunning of images based on this divine manifestation.[27]

When we relate this phrase and MacDonald's interpretation of it to our own passage in Josh 2:11, it takes on a particular significance in this new context. Particularly striking is the fact that the context of the initial use of the phrase in Deut 4:29 is essentially a command to *confess* YHWH's distinctive and intimate self-revelation to His people: "Acknowledge today and recall to mind that YHWH is God in the heavens above and upon the earth below; there is no other." Rahab, although she is a Canaanite and did not witness the speech of Moses alongside Israel, fulfills Moses' command as if she has read the book of Deuteronomy. That is to say, her phraseology is not only generally "Deuteronomic," as has long been recognized, but specifically points to YHWH's distinctive, aniconic self-revelation to Israel at Horeb. Not only does she name YHWH as Israel's God, but as Israel's *uniquely present* God, who has made Himself known in a way that distinguishes Him from all other gods (4:33–34). Included among these distinctive acts that form the background for Rahab's phrase is even the element of YHWH's separating out of Israel from Egypt to make them His own people—namely, Israel's election—to bring His promises to fulfillment and give them the land (vv. 37–38). After Rahab presents such a full and detailed account of Israel's history and its God, no wonder the spies are so quick to affirm her request for clemency!

The richness of this phrase does not end here, however. Rahab's statement stands as a pivot point between the use of the phrase in Deuteronomy and its third and final DtrH occurrence in 1 Kings 8:23, where it opens the latter part of Solomon's prayer at the dedication of the Temple. The immediate reference is to YHWH as the covenant-keeping God, obliquely recalling Horeb in its reference to YHWH's incomparability and His faithfulness to those who "walk wholeheartedly in your way" (v. 23). After addressing the topic of YHWH's equal faithfulness to His promises made to David, Solomon explores the theme of the mystery of YHWH's presence in words that evoke the pairing of heaven and earth in verse 23: "But will God really dwell on earth? The heavens, even the highest heavens, cannot contain you. How much less this Temple I have built!" (8:27). Solomon follows this statement with a series of petitions for YHWH to hear the prayers of various people who might offer their prayers to Him. Among these we find, perhaps not incidentally, a request for YHWH's openness to the prayers of those outside of Israel, so that they may come to fear Him as well (vv. 41–43).[28] Admittedly, the foreigners in question in this text come from "a distant land" to seek YHWH (v. 41), but the description of the way in which they will first encounter YHWH—"for they will hear of your great name and your mighty hand and your outstretched arm" (v. 42)—could very fittingly evoke Rahab's report of YHWH's deeds on behalf of Israel in Joshua 2:9–10. I would suggest that the way in which Rahab benefits from acknowledging YHWH's unique presence with His people—namely, the granting of her request for rescue—anticipates the way in which Solomon envisions the approach of foreigners to YHWH's dwelling place in 1 Kings 8:23. Together, this phrase laces these three texts into a chain that leads from YHWH's self-revelation to Israel at Horeb as the uniquely present God, through the astonishing confirmation of YHWH's presence by the first non-Israelite encountered in the promised land, to the invitation for foreigners to benefit from YHWH's unique dwelling among His chosen people.

The Spies' Oath and Deuteronomic Law

It is not what the spies seek from Rahab, then, but what she seeks from *them* that raises the central legal problem of the story. Rahab is unmistakably a Canaanite, to begin with. There is no doubt whatever about that. When the Israelite spies enter her house, they can hope for little more than shelter and, possibly, satisfaction. The outcome should be fairly uncomplicated: after lodging there for the necessary amount of time to complete their reconnaissance of Jericho, the spies would have packed up and returned to the Israelite camp with their report. If Rahab had turned out to be a (stereo)typical Canaanite prostitute, both her actions and those of the spies would have been relatively easy to judge. That Rahab rescues the spies, confesses YHWH, and demands an oath to preserve her life and the lives of her family raises a much more perplexing problem: namely, how should we evaluate this situation in relation to the Deuteronomic law, which requires that the Israelites "make no treaty with [the inhabitants of Canaan], and show them no mercy" (Deut 7:2)?

This question is a particularly compelling one since, as noted above, the book of Joshua is framed from the very start with reference to the "Book of the Torah" (1:8),[29] where YHWH makes clear that this "book" is to be Joshua's constant companion and guide, setting the standard for Israel's life in the land. This is one of a handful of Dtr references throughout the book of Joshua to a written form of the Law already supposed to be in Israel's possession. Within Joshua's literary and canonical context in the DtrH, we can presume that this "Book of the Torah" refers to some form of the book of Deuteronomy, by which the redactor measures Israel's activities as it enters the land. This same identification of the "Book of the Torah" seems to be assumed by those scholars who perceive a conflict between the pact with Rahab and the prohibition on covenants with the Canaanites expressed in Deuteronomy 7:2, as well as the broader corpus of commands to subject all Canaanites to the *ḥerem*—leaving "nothing alive that breathes" in their cities (Deut 20:16)—expressed in chapters 7 and 20 of Deuteronomy. Can Rahab justifiably be exempt from this apparently comprehensive decree?

To dispatch with a frequently overlooked but quite significant detail of the problem first, it should be made clear that an oath is by no means identical with a covenant, or inherently connected with a covenant. While the book of Deuteronomy sometimes uses the Niphal of *šbʿ* as a verb of covenant making[30] and while oaths often accompany covenants, both Deuteronomy and DtrH also use the language of oath apart from the context of covenants.[31] Outside of the Dtr corpus as well, the Hebrew Bible attests to numerous oaths, especially those made between individuals, that do not involve the language of covenant.[32] Assuming, then, that the spies' *oath* (*šĕbuʿa*) sworn to Rahab in Joshua 2:20 clearly violates the command in Deuteronomy 7:2 not to make *covenants* (*lōʾ-tikrōt lāhem bĕrît*) with the Canaanite nations would be a mistake.

A second challenge to this perceived conflict is that Deuteronomy addresses Israel's interactions with the Canaanites only as an idolatrous group; its laws lack instructions for dealing with individuals who do not reflect this collective identity. While Deuteronomic law gives explicit instructions on how to deal with Canaanites who, as a body, threaten to lead Israel astray, it has no place—both positively and negatively speaking—for a Canaanite who affirms YHWH and the deeds He has done on behalf of Israel. Thus, Rahab's actions and abstentions effectively challenge the applicability of the Law to the situation. How, then, should we describe the relationship between the exception made for Rahab and the laws of Deuteronomy? Here, it seems, our reading might benefit from Polzin's insight that the first few incidents in the book of Joshua serve as a "hermeneutical meditation" on the outworking of the *ḥerem*. That is, these stories delve *into* the Law, but also go beyond it in their exploration of how Israel might deal with scenarios that the Law does not directly address.[33] Read in this way, the story of Rahab fits into a gap in the Deuteronomic code, exploring how Israel deals with a situation that the Law does not directly address, and thereby providing a hermeneutical example.

A further test of the validity of the oath can be made on the basis of the consequences of this supposedly serious covenant violation: nothing happens. In the story of Achan only a few chapters later, the outcome of the *ḥerem* violation by an individual has swift and severe consequences, which mirror on a small scale the legislated punishment for an apostate Israelite city in Deuteronomy 13:12–17—particularly appropriate, even to the detail of the concluding warning, "Do not let anything designated as *ḥerem* cling to your hand . . ." On the contrary, the Rahab story hardly seems to serve as a paradigmatic illustration of the proper way of dealing with the inhabitants of Canaan in accord with Deuteronomic law. If this had been the story's purpose, it would seem no less likely that divine retribution would follow the transgression committed by two Israelites in the making of this oath. In Achan's story, punishment comes quickly on the heels of what seemed to the sinner to be a personal and hidden matter.[34] Here, however, no sign of divine wrath follows the oath that the spies make to Rahab in full view of the reader, and, as Joshua 2:23 indicates, this is fully disclosed to Joshua as well.[35] Surely Rahab's chambers are as permeable to the divine eye as the tent of Achan.

The survival of Rahab along with her kin can be contrasted not only with the person of Achan himself and with his family, however, but also with the goods he has stolen. She has in common with them that both the Canaanites and the spoils of Jericho are to be completely annihilated under the *ḥerem* command, yet some of each are instead preserved from destruction and brought into the midst of Israel. But while the heap of goods stolen by Achan betrays itself even in its hiddenness by the destruction that it brings upon Israel, Rahab and her entire family are permitted to dwell openly alongside Israel in perpetuity with no ill effects (Josh 6:25). Something, it would seem, has "defused" the *ḥerem* with regard to the household of Rahab; this outcome, in turn, seriously calls into question the illegality of the oath.

The Implications of Rahab's Exemption

How, then, does the story as it is told present its interpretation of the exception from the *ḥerem* made for Rahab? Some scholars have suggested that the account takes Rahab's confession as the primary grounds for her continued existence alongside Israel,[36] while others see the pact she makes with the spies as the essential component that exempts her from destruction.[37] Both her confession and the oath, though, seem to me to continue the same thread already spun by her actions and words on behalf of the spies, by which she proposes to weave herself into Israel's story. One way of understanding their coherence can be found in K. M. Campbell's articulation of these two elements both serving as integral parts of a covenant form that is part of the texture of the Rahab story.[38] Whether or not one agrees with Campbell that the covenant form is so explicitly present in the text, his suggestion points to the natural succession of covenant or oath to confession in the story—that is, of confession as "prologue" to and context of the oath-making.

Thus far, Rahab has confessed YHWH's power on behalf of Israel, and she has acted as an ally of Israel, implicitly acknowledging the reality she has confessed. The point at which she begins to speak of *ḥesed* is the payoff. It is not merely, as the NRSV translates it, that Rahab grounds her petition for *ḥesed* for herself and her family with "since I have dealt kindly [*ḥesed*] with you" (2:12). As Rahab's confession and her ongoing existence in perpetuity in the midst of Israel show, *ḥesed* can bear more weight in this passage. Instead of exchanging mere "kindness" for "kindness," with its soft, insubstantial resonance, Rahab is naming her action as a *merciful* one in a matter of life or death—namely, the mercy of risking her own life by harboring foreign spies and sheltering them from her fellow citizens. This, and not simple "kindness," is what makes her bold to ask for the spies' mercy in sparing her life and the lives of her family members in return: she requests life for life. By her words and actions, Rahab has allied herself to Israel insofar as she can, but now she asks the spies to grant her the right to live alongside Israel in the land as a YHWHist rather than an idolatrous threat.[39]

Once we have acknowledged the significance of Rahab's confession and the spies' acceptance of her request, it remains unclear how we should label her new relationship with Israel. Does the story depict a conversion? The acknowledgment of a God-fearer? The story of a righteous Gentile? If Rahab is not best classified as a stereotypical Canaanite, nor does she belong fully to YHWH's chosen people, then how do we appropriately understand her role in relation to Israel? Certainly, the Pentateuch offers a number of examples of non-Israelites who establish friendly attachments to Israel that are not depicted as religiously threatening.[40] So, for example, we can look back to Jethro in the book of Exodus, Tamar in Genesis, and the foreigners who remain unnamed but occasionally present in Israelite law. Outside of the Pentateuch, notable examples include Caleb (with his uncertain origin), Ruth, and Jael, all of whom act as allies of Israel. Non-Israelites like these—and, for that matter, non-Israelites in general—are merely the "non-elect," as J. Kaminsky labels them; they are not presented in the biblical texts as having an inherently negative role or fate in relation to YHWH's chosen nation, Israel.[41] The problem, however, is that the book of Deuteronomy places the nations of Canaan as a group in a more ominous category, for which Kaminsky has also supplied us with a label: that of the "anti-elect."[42] According to Kaminsky, this category is distinct from that of "the nations" and "the non-elect" in general, in that it includes only those peoples or persons who "are viewed as so evil or dangerous that warfare against them may include a call for their annihilation."[43] Since "evil" and "dangerous" are not absolute categories, I would suggest that what Kaminsky has in view is those who act to impede or frustrate YHWH's purposes for His elect.

While Kaminsky's schema offers a fair representation of the biblical text in its basic outlines, it seems to me that it neglects several significant features of the text. For one thing, his tripartite division obscures the basic division of the nations into elect—namely, Israel—and non-elect, chosen and not-chosen. Viewed this way, only the definition of the category of "elect" relates directly to YHWH's choosing, with the non-elect and the anti-elect defined only derivatively in relation to Israel's chosenness. Within the group of those who have *not* been chosen by YHWH, there is a degree of fluidity with regard to how they *relate* to YHWH and YHWH's elect. That is to say, Kaminsky's "anti-elect," those who act as "enemies of YHWH," should be distinguished as a *functional* rather than ontological category. The role of the Egyptians in relation to Israel provides a helpful illustration of this. In the case of the Exodus and Israel's bondage, Egypt in general and Pharaoh in particular are portrayed as *oppressors* of the elect rather than just neutral players in the larger historical drama.[44] At other times in Israel's history, though, Egypt hardly plays so actively antagonistic a role in relation to YHWH's purposes for Israel, and would fit quite comfortably within the category of "non-elect." This conceptualization of the "non-elect" as a group that can vary in its actions toward Israel allows one more significant possibility to spring up alongside the others that Kaminsky has offered—one that has already long existed in Jewish traditions under other labels: namely, the "pro-elect." Sometimes, certain individuals or groups among the non-elect act in ways that actively aid in and further YHWH's purposes for His elect rather than actively opposing or unwittingly ignoring them. It is in this group of the "pro-elect" that I would place the character Rahab, since she goes beyond her "non-election" by her advocacy of YHWH's people, yet remains outside the bounds of YHWH's choosing.

What Rahab as outsider *can* do, she does: she acknowledges the activity of Israel's God on behalf of Israel and, mysteriously but significantly, His self-manifestation at Horeb. Although she first acknowledges her place among those who have quailed at the report of YHWH's deeds, declaring that "a great fear has fallen on *us*" (*ʿālênû*, Josh 2:9), she precedes this acknowledgment with a bold personal confession about what *she*—in contrast to her fearful compatriots—knows to be the case: "*I* [emphasis mine] know (*yādaʿtî*) that the LORD has given this land to you . . ." (2:9). Thus, her statement places her knowledge of the deeds of YHWH before her identification with the inhabitants of Canaan; the "I" confession of YHWH's election of Israel contrasts with the "we" experience of debilitating fear.[45] This inclusion of herself among those who know the deeds of YHWH is, I think, far more significant than her unsurprising exclusion of herself from Israel. Like Ruth, she turns her back on what she has known to act in league with Israel to claim her alliance with YHWH's people.[46]

Yet further issues are raised by the idea that Rahab becomes an Israelite "convert." Some challenge the notion on the basis that her naming of YHWH to the spies as "YHWH *your* God" (emphasis mine) leaves distance between herself and Israel's God. As Nelson puts it, she remains a foreigner whose acknowledgment "underscores the self-evident power and glory of YHWH"[47] rather than expressing *her own* faithfulness to YHWH. Creach expresses even greater doubts about the weight of Rahab's confession, suggesting that Rahab's speech may characterize her only as "shrewd and discerning"[48]—more a clever strategy than an indication of changed allegiance.

These interpretations, however, both overlook the logical distinction that Rahab, even as a YHWH-honoring Canaanite, would make between herself and Israel in DtrH's words, if not her own. Her reference to YHWH as "your God" makes perfect sense in relation to the opinion of some rabbinic writers that non-Jewish proselytes should employ a similar distinction in their prayers, naming YHWH not as the "God of *our* Fathers," but as "the God of the Fathers of Israel" in private, and "the God of *your* Fathers" in the midst of the congregation (emphasis mine).[49] As these rabbis contended, YHWH is, in fact, *Israel's* God in a way that He is not Rahab's. While she may be a non-Israelite YHWHist—like Jethro, Job, and Ruth—she remains nonetheless among the non-*elect*.

On the other hand, some are troubled not so much by the question of Rahab's own words or motives as they are by the use of the language of "conversion." J. Milgrom challenges the use of such terminology as anachronistically employed with regard to this early period. He contends that "conversion" as a means of becoming incorporated into Israel is neither attested nor possible prior to the Second Temple period.[50] This controversy over the use of the language of conversion bears closer examination, since the permeability of Israel is an issue both in the book of Joshua and the book of Deuteronomy.

Excursus: Could the Canaanites Convert?

Milgrom's assertions regarding the possibility and nature of assimilation to early Israel emerge from his conversation with the work of Norman Gottwald. In his classic *The Tribes of [YHWH]*, Gottwald posits a version of Israel's formation rather different from that presented in DtrH when he argues that the growth of ancient Israel took place largely through mass conversions to YHWHism.[51] Harnessing the powerful concept of conversion in service of a social-revolutionary model of Israel's beginnings, he suggests that, far from being annihilated, many Canaanite "peasants" in fact *assimilated* into early Israel, and he includes the "Rahab group" among his examples.[52]

Jacob Milgrom, on the other hand, while appreciative of Gottwald's sociological work on the whole, argues that Gottwald's working assumption of the possibility of "conversion" in early Israel is anachronistic. According to him, conversion is not attested as a concept prior to the Second Temple period,[53] essentially after Judaism becomes a religious system that can be distinguished from Israelite national identity. Milgrom disputes Gottwald's model on the basis of P's explicit and D's implicit legal treatment of the *gēr*, the non-Israelite residing among Israel. In all cases, the *gēr* remains distinct from the people of Israel, and full assimilation to Israel occurs only through intermarriage[54]—with the obverse of this reflected in the prohibition of Israelite intermarriage with Canaanites in the *ḥerem* command of Deuteronomy 7.[55]

All of the factors playing into Gottwald's and Milgrom's disagreement are too involved to delve into here; the two actually seem to mean rather different things by the word "conversion."[56] Suffice to say that Milgrom's understanding of conversion is closer to my own, and so it is his take on the biblical portrayal of non-Israelite assimilation that will interest us most here. One factor that Milgrom's adept discussion does not seem to take into account is whether the concept of "conversion" into Israel necessarily entails full assimilation. His analysis seems to presuppose a model of conversion in which ethnic identity must necessarily be fused with adherence to a particular religious system. In the ancient world, where "church" and "state," so to speak, were woven much more tightly into a single fabric than in the modern world, we may well ask whether the two—identity within a people-group and identity within a religious system[57]—could indeed have been separable. The fact that Milgrom, though, can speak of those who confessed YHWH yet were not fully assimilated into Israel (Rahab being a relevant case in point) suggests that, in fact, ethnicity *could* be distinguished from affiliation with a particular deity. Such a presupposition is vital to his argument that non-Israelites could dwell alongside Israel *as* non-Israelites—that is, as ethnically distinct from Israel yet acknowledging YHWH. So while Milgrom is, I think, correct in arguing that "religious conversion was no factor at all in gaining admission to the Israelite people,"[58] it seems that we can at the same time acknowledge that certain non-Israelites, while not fully assimilated to Israel, are tolerated as neighbors—even Rahab, despite her people being numbered among Israel's enemies.

To sum up, I have argued that neither Rahab's identification as a Canaanite prostitute nor the spies' oath presents a genuine challenge to the faithfulness of Israel's actions. Rather, these two features of the story stand in tension with the reader's expectations in order to draw attention to YHWH's surprising activity on behalf of Israel. Upon hearing Rahab's confession, the most "obedient"—albeit unexpected—action for the spies to take vis-à-vis the book of Deuteronomy turns out to be the preservation of her life rather than her destruction.[59] Traditional interpreters were quite perceptive in emphasizing the unexpectedly positive role of Rahab as a character. Rahab's action on behalf of the spies initiated a process of demonstration and confession of her alliance with YHWH's covenant people, including even a startling allusion to YHWH's theophany at Horeb. The spies' oath, which Deuteronomic law does not directly forbid, contrary to the claims of some critical scholars, is an appropriate and merciful action in response to Rahab's mercy to them and the confession that grounds it.

Consistent with the text's portrayal of Rahab's less than complete assimilation in Joshua 6:25, we would do best to understand her continued presence in Israel's midst as fitting within the portrayal throughout the Hebrew Bible of exceptional, YHWH-acknowledging non-Israelites who dwell alongside Israel. Rahab established herself as a friend of YHWH's elect in two main ways. First, she hid the Israelite spies, thereby identifying with them and their mission in place of loyalty to her own people, and proffered this action as the grounds for her petition. We find this significantly reflected in her words to the spies that she has treated them with *ḥesed*—that is, she has treated them mercifully by sparing their lives, just as she now asks to be treated by them. By their actions, she wants the spies to reckon herself and her family as those loyal to YHWH, not as Canaanites of the sort depicted in Deuteronomy's *ḥerem* injunctions.

Second, Rahab confessed her own knowledge and acknowledgment of YHWH's power and deeds, in contrast to her own people's response of fear. This verbal action reinforces and explicates the way in which she has already acted on behalf of the spies, allying herself with YHWH and His people inasmuch as she is able. That this entire sequence and the ensuing oath are to be regarded positively is further confirmed by the spies' candid report to Joshua of "everything that had happened to them" (Josh 2:23)[60] and their assessment of the outcome of their foray as a positive sign regarding the Lord's giving of the land, based on Rahab's very own words (Josh 2:24).

In conclusion, the encounter of Rahab and the spies functions in the book of Joshua not as a story whose outcome exemplifies disobedience, but rather in terms of paradox, surprise, and subversion of appearances. What began as Israel's first and potentially risky encounter with a Canaanite, ends with the rescue of the spies by a woman who acknowledges YHWH. What at first appears to be a violation turns out, in the course of the story, to be a divine intervention, as reflected by its results in the text—a situation that, like Rahab's dwelling alongside Israel (6:25), seems to dwell alongside the Law rather than fall under its condemnation. In a surprising act of deliverance from an unexpected quarter, Israel learns anew what it means that ultimately it is YHWH's action by which Israel receives the land, and Rahab herself becomes a living and persistent reminder to Israel that the best response to YHWH's wondrous deeds on behalf of Israel is acknowledgement paired with the exercise of *ḥesed,* and that this is the response that leads to life.[61]

"Israel Has Sinned": Repentance as Obedience in the Case of Achan

Achan's sin is a clear case of Israel's transgression of YHWH's commands—perhaps the clearest in the book, since it is declared directly as such both in the words of the narrator (Josh 7:1) and in the reported words of YHWH Himself (Josh 7:11). Because of this, the story of Achan bears a different relationship to the theme of Israel's faithfulness than does the story of Rahab. Rather than posing a puzzle about how Israel should apply the Law in a doubtful situation, it illustrates the process of transgression, recognition of sin, and repentance that restores Israel to YHWH's favor. In this sense, the story of Achan is one of the most didactic portions in the book of Joshua. Particularly for the benefit of the reader, the text offers a God's-eye view of the existence of Achan's hidden crime in 7:1, even as Israel remains dangerously unaware of what has occurred and that it has become subject to divine wrath. Each component of the movement from command (Josh 6:17–19) to violation (7:1) to the discovery and resolution of Achan's disobedience (chap. 7) is clearly set out in the text, so that the reader can watch and learn from the process as it unfolds. The text strives to make the reader fully aware of exactly what is happening in this incident and why.

I would argue that the text's careful attention to detail in setting out the step-by-step progress of transgression and effect enables the story to function as a theodicy on a microcosmic level for the benefit of future generations of Israelite readers, illustrating Israel's faithful response to its discovery of Achan's hidden sin for which the whole nation had been subjected to punishment.[62] As the single most blatant and explicitly noted covenant violation in the book,[63] the story revolves around the question of how Israel is to understand disaster that befalls it when, for all appearances, it has acted in faithfulness and obedience to YHWH. Achan's sin and its aftermath function as an example of how Israel should properly recognize and respond to intentional sin committed in its midst of which it is unaware. In the fruitful resolution of this tension between apparent obedience and concealed sin, the story of Achan has several major functions in relation to later Israelite readers. First, it shows the devastating effects of "individual" sin on Israel as a whole; the entire people can experience grave consequences for the crime of one man that goes unrequited. Like the story of Rahab, this depiction introduces unexpected complications into Israel's conception of its standing before YHWH, since Israel perceives itself to have acted faithfully with regard to the ḥerem decree.

Second, through YHWH's abrupt punishment in the face of Israel's perception of its faithfulness, Israel learns first to question its own ability to live up to its covenant obligations, before jumping to the conclusion that disaster stems from YHWH's failure. Instead, the story of Achan's sin, which is notably—and remarkably—identified throughout the story as both Achan's sin *and* Israel's sin,[64] warns the Israelites to suspect themselves before they doubt YHWH. It reminds Israel that she is the more fallible covenant partner, and urges her to place confidence in YHWH before self-confidence. Additionally, disaster in this story serves as a sign of sin, a clue that Israel must seek out and punish wrongs that have been committed in its midst, even if the community as a whole has not wittingly been party to them. In sum, Israel should begin by actively seeking out its own wrongs and delivering justice when divine punishment strikes.

Third, the story demonstrates the necessity of a prompt response to sin once a transgression is recognized. The resolution must be swift if Israel is to survive before its holy God who sees and seeks out every transgression. Responsibility must be accepted and punishment executed if Israel is to stand before Him. At the same time, the story reaffirms YHWH's deep commitment to Israel even to the extent that He aids them in doing what He has commanded, leading Israel to the culprit by a process of elimination. Moving from unwitting sin to deadly resolution, the story offers Israel a theodicy in miniature, understanding Achan's crime as the explanation for the corporate disaster that follows, and offering Israel an example of how corporately to take responsibility for and make restitution for "individual" sins of which it is unaware.

The Evidence of Ai

The stunning defeat at Ai, a village occupied by a mere handful of men compared with fortified Jericho, sets up the major tension in the story—namely, what is Israel to do when apparent faithfulness is met with devastating defeat? The details of Israel's foray against Ai are painfully emphasized: in spite of the meager numbers of the inhabitants of the city—so small that the scouts who scope it out recommend sending only a contingent of Israel's full force (Josh 7:3)—Israel is routed and suffers numerous casualties at their hands (7:4–5) in place of what should have been an easy victory.[65] Through this sequence of events Israel first becomes aware that something has gone terribly awry. In response, the Israelites become like the Canaanite kings upon hearing the report of YHWH's deeds: "the heart of the people dissolved like water" (7:5). As G. Mitchell observes, this terrified response comes as a reversal of the normal pattern of the nations "fearing" in a nonreverential way in the book of Joshua.[66] Here Israel finds itself responding in a manner appropriate to YHWH's enemies rather than His elect.

This reaction is particularly appropriate in light of Joshua's interpretation of the situation in his complaint to YHWH. From his cry of distress, we can deduce that he sees the place of the Israelites and the inhabitants of the land as having been reversed. While elsewhere in the book, the Canaanites are consistently delivered into Israel's hand,[67] Joshua complains that Israel has instead been delivered into the hands of the "Amorites" (7:7). Have the tables been turned, he accuses, such that YHWH purposes to destroy *Israel* now (v. 7)? Then it would have been better for Israel to have stayed in Transjordan (v. 7)—that is, better for Israel *not* to have acted obediently in entering the land—if YHWH has not kept His promise, made on the eastern side of the river, that "no one will be able to stand against you all the days of your life" (1:7). Essentially, Joshua is accusing YHWH of abandonment, of failing to live up to His promise of presence, uniquely revealed to His people at Horeb (Deut 4:15–20) and reaffirmed to Joshua at the beginning of the book of Joshua (1:5). Not only will Israel fall prey to its enemies apart from YHWH, but YHWH's reputation will be ruined if He fails His people (7:9). To Joshua, Israel now lies as weak and helpless as the sheared Samson; all of the Canaanites will gather to defeat and destroy Israel wholesale, capitalizing on YHWH's failure (7:9). Perhaps disobedience would have been better than disaster, if YHWH does not truly keep His promises.

Some commentators rightly hear in Joshua's words an echo of the wilderness complaints, since it shares with them a wish that the previous, less risky status quo had been maintained.[68] Joshua's accusation that the Lord brought Israel into the land west of the Jordan only to kill them (Josh 7:9) parallels the wilderness generation's similar accusation regarding their fate. "It would have been better for us to serve the Egyptians than to die in the desert!" (Ex 14:12) becomes "Would that we had been content to settle beyond the Jordan!" (Josh 7:7). A curtailing of YHWH's promises begins to seem preferable to the grim prospect of abandonment in the promised land. But is Joshua's cry before the ark of the covenant, in the Lord's presence, an expression of lack of trust—a rebellious rallying cry like those uttered by the wilderness generation against their leaders—or the cry of the faithful sufferer who seeks to drive the deity to action on his behalf?

I would argue that two features of Joshua's appeal indicate that it is more than mere "grumbling." First, both the address of the complaint and the manner of its presentation argue in favor of this interpretation. Even in the midst of the betrayal and sense of abandonment that echo in Joshua's words, he still directs his plea immediately to YHWH (7:7), prostrating himself before the ark along with the elders of Israel (7:6). In contrast, all three complaints of the wilderness generation mentioned above are directed against Israel's leaders, not to YHWH: against Moses in Exodus 14:11–12 and 17:3, and against Moses and Aaron in Numbers 14:2–3. When this latter complaint is recalled in Deuteronomy 1:27, the people are described as grumbling in their tents *against* YHWH as a result of the spies' report regarding Canaan, rather than directing their complaint *to* Him.[69] In the present context, the location and position of presentation point to Joshua's cry as a demonstration of his trust in and obedience to YHWH rather than as an expression of rebellion. It is not that Joshua had turned his back on YHWH; rather, he fears that YHWH has turned His back on His people, since the evidence leads him to no other conclusion (7:8).

Second, additional support for the reading of Joshua's complaint as one grounded in faithfulness to YHWH may be derived from its overall correspondence to the lament form, as observed by commentators Butler and Nelson.[70] Both, however, note its lack of a petition; while Nelson draws no conclusion on the basis of this omission, Butler interprets it, along with the absence of a statement of trust, as transforming this lament into a "hopeless complaint against the saving acts of God."[71] I consider it more probable that the lack of a specific petition finds its basis in Joshua's ignorance of what has motivated YHWH's anger. That is, Joshua does not know *what* to ask from YHWH, since YHWH appears to have become unreliable;[72] he knows only what to *expect* of YHWH, as set out most directly to Joshua in Joshua 1. These expectations are reflected in his concluding appeal to YHWH's reputation (Josh 7:9),[73] recognizing that YHWH's actions on behalf of Israel serve as His "public face" to the rest of the nations; Israel's fate in Canaan cannot be separated from who YHWH "is." Challenging YHWH with the accusation that He has failed to keep His word to Israel, Joshua calls upon Him to be true to Himself, to act according to who He has declared Himself to be: the God who has promised His presence with Joshua and Israel (Josh 1:5, 9).[74]

YHWH's abrupt response indicates that the fault in Joshua's words lies not in their rebelliousness but in their questioning of YHWH's keeping of His promises. His sharp reply to Joshua, ordering him to his feet (v. 10), shows that grief and self-humiliation will not make up for an ill-placed confidence in Israel's obedience over YHWH's faithfulness. Instead, He straightaway declares the cause of what has occurred—"Israel has sinned; they have transgressed the covenant that I imposed on them" (v. 11)—then proceeds to detail and reiterate the nature of the crime that has taken place. He directly states this sin as the cause of Israel's defeat, against Joshua's accusations: "The children of Israel cannot rise before their enemies, turning tail before their enemies, because they have become *ḥerem*. I will not continue to be with you if you do not destroy the *ḥerem* from among you (v. 12)." YHWH clarifies that His departure from the midst of His people is the *consequence*, not the cause, of Israel's disastrous encounter at Ai. In effect, YHWH corrects the initial question that Israel should ask in response to defeat, changing it from "Why has YHWH abandoned us?" to "How have we failed to keep the covenant?" What YHWH wants from Israel is not self-abasement but action—seeking out and rectifying the wrong done.

YHWH has indicated that Israel must look to itself for the cause of YHWH's distance, and Israel proves its faithfulness by doing so. Even in the midst of His anger, YHWH demonstrates His faithfulness to the covenant and to His people by offering the remedy to His own wrath exercised in response to His people's transgression of His command regarding Jericho (7:13–15). He Himself takes the leading role in the process that will lift the *ḥerem* from Israel and restore it again to His favor, enabling the continuing fulfillment of His promises. Joshua's and Israel's subsequent obedience in carrying out the process as YHWH has instructed distinguishes them as a generation who "served the Lord." Rather than challenging YHWH's decree as the wilderness generation might have done, they accept corporate responsibility for Achan's crime.[75] This is not merely an automatic or "logical" response, but an acknowledgment of Israel's corporate character: Israel accepts that it rises and falls before YHWH as a unified entity.[76] In matters of its covenant relationship with YHWH, Israel does not distinguish between the "private" and the "public"; rather, what the individual does affects the entire people's standing. Thus, Israel demonstrates its faithfulness in that, even in the face of its defeat at Ai and its ignorance of Achan's crime, it willingly submits to YHWH's judgment with an exemplary humility and repentance. Obedient and repentant action, founded upon trust in YHWH, shows Israel truly to be faithful to the covenant and to YHWH, and makes possible the restoration of Israel's relationship with Him, enabling removal of the *ḥerem* both from Israel's midst and from upon Israel itself.[77]

To summarize, what distinguishes Israel as faithful in this situation following the divine declaration that "Israel has sinned" (7:10) is Israel's response—turning to YHWH to seek the reason for His apparent abandonment in the face of His promised presence; prompt corporate acknowledgment of responsibility for this sin, as demonstrated by acceptance of YHWH's punishment; and swift action to remove the sin from Israel's midst by taking the measures directed by YHWH. This pattern of attentiveness and responsiveness to YHWH's punishment, paired with a trust that does not allow such punishment to create a breach between Israel and its God, in spite of Israel's initial failure to comprehend the situation, is what most clearly characterizes Israel as faithful in this passage. It is the complaint of Joshua and the elders, directed immediately to YHWH in 7:6–9, which frames Israel's response in this episode. No dissenting chorus arises from the people, challenging their leaders in the manner of the wilderness generation, bidding for an abandonment of YHWH's plans at the first sign of divine absence. Instead, Joshua speaks for all Israel when he presents his challenge *to* YHWH, turning *toward* rather than away from YHWH in his distress. In this situation of apparent abandonment, faithful Israel calls YHWH to account, appealing to the promises He has made. Once the defeat is recognized as punishment, Israel acknowledges and enacts its corporate character as covenant people by accepting responsibility for Achan's transgression and seeking to eradicate the now-revealed *ḥerem* from its midst. As a result, Israel's restoration to YHWH's favor, as manifested by its successful second strike at Ai (Josh 8), testifies not only to YHWH's covenant faithfulness—now proved true against Joshua's challenge—but to Israel's as well.

A Traitor Within and an Ally Without

In this pair of stories, Israel finds YHWH's mercy unexpectedly delivered through a Canaanite prostitute who responds to YHWH's deeds with awe rather than fear, and encounters a lesson about YHWH's justice and Israel's repentance as Achan's theft thrusts him and all Israel under the ban. These two exceptional cases end with a Canaanite and her family preserved by one woman's advocacy of Israel, and an Israelite family destroyed by the greed that led one man to become a law breaker. By these stories and the tensions they raise, Israel learns to look for YHWH's action on its behalf in surprising places and by surprising means, whether through the protection afforded in a house of ill repute in Jericho, unexpectedly providing assurance of YHWH's presence with Israel and His gift of the land, or through an unexpectedly devastating defeat that reveals sin and enables the restoration of YHWH's presence and protection. Through surprise and subversion of appearances, these stories present an unlikely heroine without and an unseen villain within, teaching Israel to place its trust in YHWH's faithfulness as exhibited both in His mercy and in His justice.

THREE

The Gibeonites and the Transjordanian Altar

The stories of the Gibeonite deception and the Transjordanian altar do not exhibit the natural connection inherent in Rahab's and Achan's ties to the conquest of Jericho, and thus are not commonly studied side by side as are Rahab and Achan. Yet they share a key feature: in both stories, Israel finds itself having to navigate a dilemma of faithfulness to YHWH without any immediate word of divine guidance. In the case of the Gibeonite covenant, Israel must come to terms with its own guilt without an accusation from above, then must struggle to take responsibility for its error rather than succumb to the temptation to violate its oath-confirmed covenant with the crafty Gibeonites. The Transjordanian altar incident, on the other hand, depicts an intra-Israelite puzzle of obedience, as Israel, at last given rest from its enemies in the land, must struggle with what it means to remain united around YHWH even as the tribes disperse to their own territories—a dilemma embodied by the massive and dubious altar constructed by the Transjordanians.

These dilemmas of faithfulness are distinctively framed in that YHWH does not directly intervene in either situation, whether by word or deed.[1] In neither story does Israel have an external indicator of YHWH's displeasure, such as failure in battle or a divinely sent blight, to reveal its sin as it did in the case of Achan. Instead, both situations require Israel to draw upon its prior knowledge of YHWH and His Law, joined with an honest recognition of Israel's own weaknesses gleaned from its history of error and repentance. Given this divine reticence, these stories are perhaps most remarkable for the process of Israel's reaction and deliberation which they portray. In the first, a hasty initial judgment leads Israel into a binding action that it will come to regret, while in the second story, the initial judgment of the Cisjordanian tribes gives way to a more thorough investigation that forestalls a tragic outcome. Through the working out of these dilemmas, Israel learns to rely on YHWH's past revelation of His character and His Law in the present experience of divine silence. Israel continues to grow into YHWH's high calling of election as it grows in the knowledge of its own fallibility and of the mercy it has itself received, and in the process, learns to dispense mercy and justice with humility.

The Gibeonite Deception: Erring, and Erring on the Side of Mercy

Background to the Gibeonite Deception

"Do not be afraid; do not be discouraged" (Josh 8:1): YHWH's exhortation to Joshua as he prepares for the second Israelite attempt to conquer Ai, recalls similar words in Joshua's commissioning at the outset of the book (Josh 1:9). Just as the Lord promised then that Joshua would achieve unmitigated victory ("No one will be able to stand up against you all the days of your life," 1:5), He assures Joshua of the defeat of Ai in advance ("I have delivered into your hands the king of Ai, his city, his people, and his land," 8:1). These similarities convey to

Joshua and to the reader that the situation has returned to normal after Achan's crime, and YHWH's favor is with Israel once more. The removal of Achan's household and his stolen goods from Israel's midst has effectively lifted the ban from Israel, so that Israel's next foray into Ai is as successful as the first was disastrous. A heap of stones marking the grave of the king of Ai, which exists "to this day" (8:29), recalls Achan's mound, which also "remains to this day" (7:26).[2] Both serve as reminders of obedience—signs that Israel has done as the Lord commanded—and warnings to future generations about rebellion against YHWH.

Now follows a cultic interlude in Joshua 8:30–35, akin to the much more lush and extravagant portrait provided of the Jordan River crossing in Joshua 4–5, offering a "miniature" portrait of obedience. At the close of chapter 8, a stone structure is raised just as the stones were heaped up at the Jordan; its construction in accord with the Lord's commands given through Moses, recorded in the "book of the Law" (vv. 30–31), highlights that it is attentiveness to the Law and commandments that characterizes 8:30–35. Everything that is done in this section of cultic and legal observance is done carefully and legitimately, and in the presence of all Israel. In addition to the altar, built according to the Mosaic prescription, Joshua inscribes the Law on stones as Israel looks on (v. 32). Then, the whole assembly proceeds to call out the blessings and curses from Ebal and Gerizim, again "as Moses the servant of the Lord had formerly commanded" (v. 33). At the close of the scene, Joshua reads the entire book of the Law aloud to the people,[3] and the text places a particular emphasis on the *completeness* of this act: "There was not a word of all that Moses had commanded that Joshua did not read to the whole assembly of Israel . . ." (v. 35). The text makes the reader acutely aware that Israel's corporate memory of its covenant obligations has been thoroughly refreshed.

This reiteration of Israel's corporate awareness of and attentiveness to the Law has a double purpose, however. Read in the context of what precedes, it highlights the obedient propagation of the Law on the part of Joshua, as the bearer of Moses' legacy, and the presence and participation of the entire community ("including the women and children, and the aliens who lived among them," v. 35) in this concern for and awareness of the Law. In light of the story that follows in chapter 9, however, this verse sets up a sharply ironic contrast between Israel's focused, corporate hearing of and obedience to the Law at Mount Ebal—every word, as reiterated in both verses 34 and 35!—and its carelessness in pursuing the Law's application with regard to the Gibeonite treaty.[4]

The Successful Ruse of the Gibeonite Commission

While Rahab made a bid for her life by deceiving her fellow Canaanites in a demonstration of ḥesed toward Israel, the Gibeonites seek to preserve their lives by deceiving *Israel*. Posing as a delegation that has traveled from a great distance to make peace with Israel, they abruptly request a treaty (9:3). To the Israelites' credit, they respond with a question based on their recent review of the Law, recalling the Deuteronomic prohibition on treaties with their neighbors in the land: "But perhaps you live near us; how then can we make a treaty with you?" (v. 4). Though unnamed here, the book of the Law is implied and recalled in this question as latently present in the background of the story, always at hand for Israel's guidance. Israel can only recognize the possibility of a violation because it knows of a commandment to violate: no neighboring peoples present in the land are to be spared, but rather all are to be subjected to the ḥerem (Deut 7:1–6 and 20:16–18). Based upon its awareness of this law, Israel will stand condemned by its own mouth as soon as it becomes aware that the Gibeonites live only a stone's throw away. Persuaded by the ruse for the time being—just as the goat skins on Jacob's arms persuaded the blind Isaac—the men of Israel accept verification of the staleness of the travelers' bread as sufficient evidence, and Joshua promptly grants the commission a peace treaty, which the Israelite leaders affirm with an oath (vv. 14–15).

Here, significantly, the distinction made between oath and covenant in our discussion of the Rahab story comes into play; Joshua makes peace with Gibeon precisely through making "a covenant with them to preserve their lives," thereafter ratified by the "leaders of the congregation" (9:15). This covenant does not slip quietly between the Deuteronomic prohibitions as the oath to Rahab does, but instead glaringly violates them. First, it clashes with the prohibition on covenant-making with the Canaanite peoples in Deuteronomy 7:2, and second, it directly evokes the distinction between the treatment of near and distant cities in Deuteronomy 20:10–18 through the Israelites' challenge to the Gibeonites' initial claim of proximity (Josh 9:6–7). Despite Israel's attempts to verify the Gibeonites' claims—substantiated by the carefully and cleverly falsified signs of a long journey—the text informs us that the Israelites have neglected to make what is perhaps the most crucial inquiry: "they did not inquire of the mouth of YHWH" (v. 14).

Three days later, when the truth is somehow discovered,[5] Israel sets off immediately for the Gibeonite cities (vv. 17–18) with unclear purpose. This swift trip northward to confront the deceivers belies the painfully fresh memory of the consequences of *herem* violation Israel has so recently witnessed in the person of Achan. In addition, perhaps it evokes also the memory of the covenant curses Israel recited not long ago at Mount Gerizim, in Joshua 8.[6] At first, the outlook is not good. The people begin dangerously to resemble the wilderness generation in their grumbling against their leaders for sealing the treaty with an oath before YHWH, which now binds their hands (9:18); Israel would prefer to have license to deal with the Gibeonites as they originally should have done according to the *herem* commands.[7]

Israel's inaction points to its realization that it cannot simply take its revenge against Gibeon by reverting to the *herem* command, as if this could still constitute "obedience."[8] The central dilemma of the story now arises: while keeping the oath they have made to the Gibeonites is in tension with the command to subject its near neighbors in Canaan to the *herem*, the Israelites cannot commit the Gibeonites to *herem* now without violating the oath they have made by YHWH to preserve the lives of the Gibeonites (v. 18). Like Jephthah's vow and its heavy consequences in Judges 11:30, 34–36, Israel cannot escape the obligation that it has rashly taken upon itself without "wrath" falling upon it as a consequence (Josh 9:20).

But what *should* be done—what constitutes a faithful action in dealing with this sin? The proper response to the treaty-making is by no means as clear-cut as the sin of making the treaty. In contrast to

Achan's hidden sin, whose consequences and resolution soon became readily apparent to all Israel, this time all Israel has participated in the sin through its leaders, in full public view, but the proper response of the community once the sin is realized remains obscure and uncertain. Achan and his family could be singled out and eradicated as a danger to the community, but corporate sin cannot be so easily isolated and removed. Yet Israel knows that it must be dealt with, or a far worse recompense from YHWH will soon follow.

As for YHWH Himself, He remains silent. In contrast to His vocal participation in the identification of Achan after the defeat at Ai, He offers no direct guidance or address to the situation. He neither points out the transgression nor supplies its punishment. Within the story, His silence seems to correspond to Israel's failure to inquire of Him, as stated in Joshua 9:14; just as His speaking answered Joshua's petitionary challenge at the start of chapter 7, His silence answers Joshua's silence here. Instead, the process of sin, recognition, and response in this story—in marked contrast to the story of Achan—takes place entirely "on the ground." Israel is learning, through this episode, how to come to terms with its own sin even in the absence of a divine reprimand.[9]

"A Word Fitly Spoken": The Speech of the Leaders

The speech of Israel's leaders fills this gap of speechlessness, supplying the solution even as the massed Israelites seethe outside Gibeon's gates. The turning point of Israel's faithfulness in the story occurs here, at last joining this story of *ḥerem*-dodging with the story of Achan's *ḥerem*-violation, since the crucial step for resolution is the same: the recognition of what Israel has done. This comes through clearly in the leaders' statements about the inviolability of the oath they have made, as they repentantly shift the focus from the deception that the Gibeonites have perpetrated to Israel's own part in the illicit treaty-making: "We have given them our oath by the Lord, the God of Israel, and we cannot touch them now" (9:19). Employing the first-person plural, they point to Israel's covenant obligations, what "we have given them" (v. 19), as what is really at issue, not Gibeon's offense—or even the leaders' own offense, as the people see it—against Israel. They refuse to act upon the people's chafing against the oath, recognizing that the initial failure of the Israelites to judge wisely cannot be undone.[10] Violation of a treaty oath made before the Lord will itself constitute a transgression at this point, bringing "wrath" upon Israel, rather than restoring the original situation (v. 20).[11]

Instead, the leaders' solution urges the people to exercise the same sort of difficult covenant faithfulness that YHWH has exhibited toward Israel thus far, even though this mercy is undeserved by the Gibeonites just as it is unmerited by Israel. In contrast to Rahab, the Gibeonites have not treated the Israelites with *ḥesed*, instead securing a treaty through trickery that jeopardizes Israel. Yet Israel as treaty partner accepts that it is bound by the treaty and acts with *ḥesed* for its part.[12] At the same time that this act carries a certain measure of mercy, though, the leaders enable the treaty to serve as *punishment* for both parties: Israel accepts the consequences of its actions by adhering to the terms of preservation agreed to, while lowering Gibeon's status from treaty partner to bond servant—thereby dealing with Israel's sin and Gibeon's in one package.

For Israel's part, its punishment is that it must forever share the promised land, never to be completely separated from the nations. Even if Israel perfectly carried out the *ḥerem* command in relation to every other Canaanite in the land, the Gibeonites would remain forever in the land alongside Israel because of this failing on Israel's part. The family of Rahab was small enough to be assimilated, or at least to stand as an exception. But now the Gibeonites, an entire people-group, have been bound to Israel forever in a way that changes their relationship to Israel and Israel's relationship to them. Israel has taken on covenant obligations not only in relation to YHWH, but to the nations. This might be a small enough burden, if it did not bear with it more ominous echoes in the larger scheme of the book, as the ongoing presence of Canaanites continues to be emphasized alongside Israel's failure to occupy the land.[13]

As for the Gibeonites, they get more than they bargained for: while they sought their lives (9:3–4) and offered themselves as "servants" to

Israel (v. 11), they are sentenced to lives of service to YHWH. This is an ironic twist, in that while Rahab first confessed YHWH and openly expressed her knowledge of the *ḥerem* and only secondarily asked for her life, the Gibeonites conceal a primary interest in self-preservation by using their report of YHWH's deeds to serve this end. Initially, the Gibeonites presented a speech similar to Rahab's, extolling YHWH's deeds on behalf of Israel (vv. 9–11), suggesting that it was His reputation that brought them to make peace with Israel. But unlike Rahab, they spoke only of the battles across the Jordan, *prior* to Israel's entrance into Canaan (9:10–11). This curious omission of YHWH's deeds within the land of Canaan has one meaning in the context of the Gibeonites' speech, and another meaning in relation to the reader. First, it serves in the Gibeonites' deception to suggest that they had heard the report of YHWH's deeds and set out on their conciliatory journey some time ago, and are therefore unaware of more recent events surrounding Israel's arrival in the land. Second, the omission, by avoiding reference to Israel's latest conquests, calls the reader's attention to another level of the deception, which is not apparent to Israel: that in fact the primary instigation for their journey is not the report of YHWH's fame, but "what Joshua had done to Jericho and Ai" (Josh 9:3), knowledge that the reader has been privy to from the outset of the story. As the Gibeonites indeed admit in answer to Joshua's question about their motives, they acted not so much out of reverence for YHWH as out of a more immediate fear of *ḥerem* (v. 34).[14]

Thus, the modification Joshua makes to the sentence the leaders have passed binds the Gibeonites in permanent allegiance to and service of YHWH. Instead of relegating the Gibeonites to mere servitude, Joshua requires them to act as hierodules, binding them permanently to the sanctuary of YHWH Himself. The revised sentence that Joshua passes recognizes the sin as an unfaithful act not only toward Israel, as wronged treaty partner, but also against YHWH, whom Gibeon initially—falsely—hailed, and to whom it is now inevitably attached through Israel, whether or not it intended to be. In so doing, Joshua acknowledges that both the deception and Israel's action in making the treaty are primarily a crime against YHWH, and transfers Gibeon's service to the One to whom it is due rather than to Israel. This attachment to YHWH's cult in particular, rather than simply bondage to menial service of Israel, suggests that it was YHWH in His role as overlord or suzerain who should have been consulted before an act of treaty-making took place between His vassal Israel and *any* people-group, Canaanite or otherwise, appearances notwithstanding. At the same time, Joshua's decision strikingly comes as close as possible to carrying out the original sentence against these Canaanites. His modified sentence subjects the Gibeonites to a sort of "living *ḥerem*," in effect, dedicated to YHWH for life-long service rather than dedicated by destruction.[15] Before we can fully understand this resolution of Israel's relationship with Gibeon, we must further explore the concept of the *ḥerem*.

Excursus: The *Ḥerem*

The *ḥerem* commands in the book of Deuteronomy and the practice of *ḥerem* in the book of Joshua and a handful of other biblical texts have long proved vexing for readers of the Hebrew Bible. Granted, the fact that a few readers in the Bible's long history have eagerly seized upon these texts to justify their own deeds of violence has only magnified the problem.[16] For the most part, however, readers in the modern world have been most concerned with curtailing the exploitation of these texts by those who would manipulate them for their own ends, or at least to rid us once and for all of the notion that these shocking texts should continue to function in any positive way as Scripture for modern communities of faith. Those who do continue to read these texts within faith communities often experience a similar repugnance toward the divine command to depopulate the land of Canaan and wonder what, exactly, these uncomfortable texts are doing in their Bibles.

The reality that critical scholars and religious readers alike still struggle with these texts suggests that there is no easy solution to be found. I think, however, that we can understand these texts significantly better by clarifying the questions that we bring to them. Too often discussions of the *ḥerem* inadvertently muddle together the issues involved, and thus reach only a partial resolution that allows one text or another to slip through the cracks and leaves some dimension or other of the problem still unresolved. As a result, I propose that the "problem" of the *ḥerem* must be disassembled into its component parts, so that each can be properly addressed on its own terms and none inadvertently omitted. Only in this way can a genuinely satisfactory understanding of one of the most troubling quandaries of biblical criticism and biblical faith be reached.

Historical Dimensions

To begin with the barest historical facts, we must set out with the awareness that ancient Israel was a nation or at least a people-group—that is to say, a political entity—along with a sensitivity to the implications of this identification. This leads us to address the preconceptions and prejudices that we bring as modern readers to the *ḥerem* metaphor. Even scholarly readers who should know better often mistakenly treat the *ḥerem* commands anachronistically, as if we were dealing with a period when religion could be extricated from the political order. Yet in this way, ancient Israel did not differ from other political entities of its time. Religious beliefs had not yet been extricated from the public realm and relegated by the Enlightenment to private practice and individual choice.[17] Rather, they were part of the essential *shape* of communities, woven into the very fabric of their existence; nations and gods inherently belonged together in a sort of supernatural matchmaking.[18] While this may seem obvious to critical readers, its full implications for Israel's practice of *ḥerem* often goes unnoticed. K. Lawson Younger's study of ancient conquest accounts provides a sweeping survey of the extreme language of conquest—language that by its very nature employs exaggeration and overstatement as tools of self-presentation.[19] In the cultural and political context of the ancient Near East, the Israelite conception of *ḥerem* was neither unique, as we know from the Mesha Inscription, nor even much different from the rhetoric of annihilation employed by other ancient Near Eastern cultures in advertising their victories.[20] To begin with, then, we must understand that within its historical and political context, the language of *ḥerem* may have been forceful, but it was certainly not aberrant. The idea may have been frightening to those targeted by this rhetoric of violence—just as Egyptian or Assyrian threats of violence would have been[21]—but not uniquely horrendous or unthinkable.

The necessary starting point for analyzing the *ḥerem* texts, it seems to me, is the admission that the problem with the texts is, in part, a modern one. As I have pointed out elsewhere,[22] the only reason scholars express so much concern about the religio-military ethos and practices depicted in the biblical texts is that communities of faith still use those texts today. Brutal as one may find the Assyrians, for example, no one cares much to evaluate the ethical challenges posed by their atrocities, since virtually no reader today turns to the Assyrian records as a source of their religious beliefs. Whether or not modern scholarship realizes how inextricably its concerns about the moral implications of the *ḥerem* commands are linked with the hermeneutics and practice of modern communities of faith, this acknowledgment is a vital part of how we understand what so worries us about these texts. As a result, even scholars who have no religious attachment to these texts, and are not themselves seeking to put these texts into practice, have a vested interest in exploring and understanding how these texts might be appropriately acted upon by faithful readers.

While historical differences in assumptions about communication form part of the problem, a second set of historical conventions helps to put these texts in proper perspective—namely, the conventions governing the rhetoric of warfare and violence in the historical context out of which the texts arise. If we accept that what these texts say would not have been considered aberrant within their historical context of origin, we have come that much closer to understanding the *ḥerem* motif rather than merely being repelled by it. Given this historical awareness, it becomes obvious that the meaning and motivation of these texts do not lie in a unique bloodthirstiness among the Israelites in general or the Deuteronomists in particular, but, as we will explore further below, in a deep concern for the unmitigated allegiance to YHWH upon which Israel's very existence depends.

Next, it is helpful to recognize the development of the concept of *ḥerem* as reflected in the biblical texts and assisted by comparison with the Mesha Inscription.[23] Initially, it appears that the Israelite practice of *ḥerem* originated as a vow made by Israel or as a command issued by YHWH pertaining to a *particular situation*.[24] For example, the complete destruction of the city of Arad originates in an occasion-specific vow made by the Israelites in response to the capture of several of their number by the inhabitants of this city (Num 21:1–3). In 1 Samuel 15:1–3 as well, Saul's responsibility of committing all of the Amalekites and their goods to the *ḥerem* turns on a situationally specific divine command that functions here as the vow does in Numbers 21. The implications are the same in both cases: the devotion by destruction of all living things in the context in question is to be complete, but the *ḥerem* extends no further than the immediate event. Similarly, the Mesha Stele recounts at least one such occasional vow made by King Mesha in the course of his battles against Israel, dedicating the town of Nebo to Ashtar-Chemosh.[25] Notably, not every city that he attacks is dealt with in this way; complete destruction appears to be reserved for the city that Mesha presents as an offering, since the inscription mentions the rebuilding of other Israelite cities that he captures. It appears, then, that the *ḥerem* begins not as a unilateral military policy, but as an action that turns on a single, occasion-specific commitment to a deity.

Literary Development

From this starting point, the Deuteronomistic historians adopt the historic practice of *ḥerem* as a narrative motif, and in the process, imbue it with new content and meaning. In DtrH, *ḥerem* comes to designate Israel's standard policy in the conquest of its near neighbors in the land of Canaan, shifting from an occasional vow to a blanket injunction covering all cities within the land that YHWH has promised to Israel.[26] This development results in the frequent and distinctive use of *ḥerem* terminology in Dtr writings[27]—particularly in the book of Joshua, which contains about half of the occurrences within DtrH of words derived from this root. Although this prevalence of *ḥerem* language is chiefly a literary move, as its late advent and combination with earlier texts that assume Canaanite survival show, the frequency of Dtr's use of *ḥerem* means that the distinctive Dtr reframing of this concept—artificial though it may be—dominates the usage of these terms in the Hebrew Bible.

Both in the book of Joshua and elsewhere, the language of *ḥerem* forms a perceptible overlay on pre-Dtr texts, sometimes meshing awkwardly with alternative accounts of Israel's dealings with the Canaanites.[28] The Dtr origin of this particular application of *ḥerem* language becomes particularly evident when DtrH employs this language even where it is absent from parallel stories in other sources. For example, in recounting Israel's conquest of the territories belonging to Sihon and Og, DtrH repeatedly speaks of Israel's actions in terms of *ḥerem*,[29] since Israel is taking lands that YHWH has given it as its inheritance. Yet *ḥerem* language is notably absent from E's account of the destruction of Sihon's and Og's territories in Numbers 21:21–35—a contrast in terminology that is thrown into even sharper relief by Israel's enactment of a spontaneous *ḥerem* vow in relation to Arad earlier in the same chapter (vv. 1–3).[30] The use of *ḥerem* language for Israel's conquest of Sihon and Og in Deuteronomy and Joshua compared with its absence from the same context in Numbers demonstrates the shift in usage of the root *ḥrm* that takes place in DtrH. From its prior incidental usage in relation to a specific dedicatory situation, DtrH broadens and adapts it as the standard mode of Israel's military activity in the course of its conquest of the land YHWH has given.

Usage and Meaning in the Deuteronomistic History

Why, though, did DtrH choose to seize upon this earlier military practice as a literary motif? Critical scholars continue to struggle to comprehend the choice of such a bloody ideal, even if this sweeping "*ḥerem* policy" was never actually put into practice. Fortunately, R. W. L. Moberly and his student Nathan MacDonald point us in an appropriate direction to seek an answer to this question, through their reading of Deuteronomy 7 as an explication of the Shema.[31] For MacDonald, building on Moberly's initial insight,[32] the application of the *ḥerem* to all Canaanites corresponds to Israel's acknowledgment of YHWH as its only God and Lord in the face of competing claims to deity and lordship: it functions as the *negative counterpart* to Israel's single-minded and wholehearted devotion to YHWH.[33] In other words, just as closely as Israel clings to YHWH as its One Holy Lord, it is to distance itself from, even anathematize, all that is unholy—essentially, all that is "not-YHWH"—that competes for its allegiance in the land.

MacDonald follows Moberly in arguing that the statement of *ḥerem* in Deuteronomy 7:1–2 is further limited and defined by the commands that follow it in vv. 3–4, both of which assume the ongoing presence of Canaanites in the land.[34] As Moberly puts it, "Whatever the 'literal' implementation of *ḥerem* in certain Old Testament narratives might appear to mean, and whether or not *ḥerem* was ever actually implemented in Israel's warfare, Deuteronomy 7, I suggest, presents *ḥerem* as a metaphor for religious fidelity which has only two primary practical expressions, neither of which involve the taking of life."[35] According to Moberly's and MacDonald's views, these verses set out the way in which Israel is to enact the *ḥerem*—not through mass execution, but by refraining from intermarriage with Canaanites and by destroying their cult objects. Both the abstention and the action, the negative and the positive command, share the same goal of preventing Israel from swaying in its allegiance to YHWH by entering into idolatry.[36] Thus, Moberly and MacDonald conclude that the commands in Deuteronomy 7:3–4 that follow the use of *ḥerem* language in verse 2 signal that the *ḥerem* command functions here *metaphorically* rather than literally—not as "mere metaphor," Moberly reminds, but rather actualized through commands that express Israel's exclusive devotion to YHWH without the taking of life.[37]

The promise held out by such a reading becomes apparent from Moberly's next few sentences, as he writes, "If this understanding is on the right lines, then usage of *ḥerem* terminology elsewhere in Deuteronomy (e.g., 20:16–18) is not a problem. For once it is grasped that the term functions as a metaphor for religious faithfulness, then all injunctions are interpreted accordingly."[38] Thus, Moberly proposes taking the *ḥerem* text in Deuteronomy 7:2–4 as paradigmatic for the use of *ḥerem* language within Deuteronomy and presumably throughout the Deuteronomistic corpus. Such a reading effectively redirects the force of the metaphor toward fulfillment in ardent love of YHWH and two specific applications of this, rather than toward wholesale slaughter. In Moberly's and MacDonald's reading, therefore, the *ḥerem* of the Canaanites is actualized *solely* by destruction of their cultic paraphernalia and refraining from intermarriage with them, both of which actions prevent Israel's contact with their idolatrous ways.[39] Consequently, Josiah's destruction of illicit cult objects becomes for both scholars the quintessential act of the practical implementation of the *ḥerem* as an outgrowth of the Shema, effectively situating the *ḥerem* motif within the first edition of DtrH.[40]

Yet this interpretation of the *ḥerem* is difficult to sustain once the content of other *ḥerem* texts in Deuteronomy and DtrH is taken into account.[41] Neither study fully accounts for the challenge that Deuteronomy's own usage outside of chapter 7 presents to Moberly's initial conclusions regarding the meaning of *ḥerem* language. As a result, neither study takes into account how this might affect the dating and significance of both Deuteronomy's and DtrH's application of *ḥerem* language overall.[42] I will argue that, based upon the full range of texts in Deuteronomy and DtrH that employ *ḥerem* language, we cannot so easily dismiss the violence of the metaphor. Instead, we must understand it as an exilic rhetorical strategy directed at understanding Israel's punishment for its idolatry rather than as a polemic directed at a Canaanite "other."

First, we will deal with the challenge that other texts within Deuteronomy present to the theory of *ḥerem* as metaphor. The root *ḥrm* occurs in five other contexts in Deuteronomy, twice before chapter 7 (2:34; 3:6), twice as a noun at the end of chapter 7 (vv. 26, two uses), and twice after chapter 7 (13:16, 18; 20:17). Although only one of these occurrences (20:17) applies the verb to the original inhabitants of Canaan, it seems appropriate to survey the range of usage across the book before arriving at firm conclusions about its meaning in any given context.

In the first two instances, the subjects of the ḥerem are the inhabitants of the kingdoms of Og and Sihon on the east side of the Jordan. Here, the range of application of ḥerem is specified. In Deuteronomy 2:34, the ḥerem applied to Sihon's kingdom includes "men, women, and children," with the additional reinforcing observation that "we left no survivors." Og's kingdom is said to have been similarly subjected to the ḥerem, with an explicit comparison to Sihon's; the full inclusion of "men, women, and children" under the ḥerem again receives mention (3:6), and the lack of survivors among Og's army (3:3) provides a parallel to the lack of a remnant in 2:34. Livestock and plunder from all cities in these campaigns are noted to have been exempt from the ḥerem (3:7).

In a twist of divine justice, it is the apostate Israelite city that finds itself subject to the ḥerem in Deuteronomy 13:13–18.[43] In this case—unlike that of Sihon and Og—even livestock is included within the application of the ḥerem to living inhabitants of the city (13:15). Likewise, the material contents of the city and the city itself are not to benefit Israel but are to be given over completely and permanently to YHWH by fire—so much so, that the city must "remain a ruin forever" (13:16). The reason given for these actions is significant: Israel must put as much distance as possible between itself and these things subjected to ḥerem, because these things incur the Lord's wrath (v. 17) and are contrary to Israel's life as YHWH's obedient people (v. 18). Whether the threat to stray from YHWH comes from without or within, Israel is to resist it with equal vehemence. Using the noun ḥerem twice, Deuteronomy 7:26 makes the same point in an even more direct way: if Israel takes in any of the Canaanite cult objects devoted to ḥerem, Israel likewise will be reckoned as ḥerem.

Finally, the application of ḥerem language to the nations of Canaan in Deuteronomy 20:16–18 distinguishes it as the only other text in Deuteronomy to do so outside of chapter 7.[44] The language of ḥerem is used in this instance to distinguish Israel's disassociation from its near neighbors in Canaan from Israel's potentially friendly relations with more distant cities (cf. 20:10–15). In contrast to the possibility of forming a treaty with these other cities or at least sparing the lives of all inhabitants besides adult males, Israel is commanded with regard to the Canaanite cities: "Do not leave alive anything that breathes" (20:16). This destruction serves primarily as a deterrent to Israel's own straying, disobedience, and ultimate destruction (v. 18). Furthermore, this subjection of the Canaanites to *ḥerem* itself fulfills a divine command and is requisite to Israel's obedience (v. 17).

What this survey of *ḥerem* language within the book of Deuteronomy shows is that every use of *ḥerem* language outside of chapter 7 *explicitly mentions* the slaughter of living things in association with the *ḥerem*—whether by the listing of "men, women, and children" along with the note on the lack of survivors in 2:34 and 3:6, or by indicating the totality of slaughter with descriptions such as putting to the sword "all that is in [the city]" (13:15) or slaying "everything that breathes" (20:16). How, then, does this specification of killing as part of the *ḥerem* relate to the use of *ḥerem* language in Deuteronomy 7? We could begin by classifying the first two incidences of *ḥerem* in the book as belonging to the "traditional" form and meaning of *ḥerem*—namely, the incidental vow that entails the elimination of all living things in a city. The treatment of the apostate Israelite city in Deuteronomy 13 mirrors the way in which Israel is to deal with Canaanite cities, with the added severity of forbidding the taking of any livestock or material plunder.[45] Contamination, rather than dedication, seems to be the primary concern of the implementation of *ḥerem* in this case. None of these occurrences thus far directly relates to the comprehensive *ḥerem* applied to the Canaanites in Deuteronomy 7.

The final—and closest—parallel found in Deuteronomy 20, however, is a different matter. As the only text in Deuteronomy besides chapter 7 that speaks of the *ḥerem* applied to the inhabitants of Canaan, it complicates a metaphorical understanding of Deuteronomy 7 significantly. Instead of speaking of the *ḥerem* in terms of the destruction of cult objects or bans on intermarriage, as it could be understood in 7:2–4, it specifies the slaughter of "everything that breathes" (20:16)!

Similarly, in the summary of the conquest of Canaan found in chapters 10 and 11 of Joshua, which repeatedly emphasizes Joshua's fulfillment of the commands given through Moses, the text similarly pairs *ḥerem* terminology with declarations of the elimination of "everything that breathes" (10:40; 11:11, 14).

In sum, the broader corpus of Deuteronomic *ḥerem* passages resists a comfortable fit within Moberly's and MacDonald's interpretation of Deuteronomy 7:3–5 as paradigmatic for how Deuteronomy envisions the *ḥerem* being put into practice, and thereby points to the need for a modification of their understanding of the *ḥerem* metaphor. Whether or not the *ḥerem* as destruction of all living things in a city actually occurred in Israel's interactions with Canaan, the fact remains that the majority of texts in Deuteronomy that use *ḥerem* language do indeed *command* and *depict* the implementation of the *ḥerem* in terms of wholesale slaughter. The application of the *ḥerem* depicted in the book of Joshua only compounds the challenge presented by the other texts in Deuteronomy, exhibiting a notable absence of the concerns about intermarriage and destruction of cult objects that Moberly's and MacDonald's interpretation would lead us to expect. Instead, it confronts us with an explicit association of the *ḥerem* with complete destruction and slaughter in the case of Jericho in Joshua 6, as well as numerous examples in the campaign summary statements of Joshua 10–11, which repeatedly associate it with a lack of survivors, and seem to serve as the fulfillment of the Deuteronomic commands.[46] This suggests that a full understanding of the *ḥerem* of the Canaanites—even as metaphor—must somehow incorporate the violent dimension found in so many texts associated with it.

A Double-Edged Metaphor

Taking the image of violent destruction as an intrinsic part of the *ḥerem* metaphor would require a few key modifications to Moberly's and MacDonald's assumptions and conclusions. First, the origin of the blanket application of *ḥerem* of the Canaanite nations as a Dtr *literary motif* plays a crucial role in defusing its genocidal tone. The inability of

Israel to apply this command to any actual Canaanites at the time of its creation is far more than a historical aside; rather, it becomes the key for unlocking the meaning of this harsh language. Second, with the Canaanites out of the picture, the violent thrust of this metaphor seeks a target—and finds it in Israel itself, as demonstrated by the analogy between Israel and the destroyed nations in Deuteronomy 8:19–20 and the *ḥerem* of the idolatrous city in Deuteronomy 13:12–18. The meaning and logic of the *ḥerem* of the Canaanites becomes clear when its innovation is attributed not to the time of Josiah—as both Moberly and MacDonald presume,[47] and as R. Nelson and L. Rowlett have argued at greater length[48]—but to an exilic redaction of DtrH.[49] Read within this context, Israel's full devotion to YHWH and shunning of idolatry is one point of the *ḥerem*; depiction of the *consequences that will befall Israel in the land*, should it fail to give its full allegiance to YHWH, is the other. Both the loss of the land and the means of its avoidance, the possibility of obedience and the consequences of disobedience, are held together within the metaphor of the *ḥerem*.

We will begin by making a case for the dating of Dtr's distinctive use of *ḥerem* language to a post-Josianic stratum of the history—a move that radically affects its meaning—then further explicate the function of this language within the Dtr corpus. Scholars generally attribute the conceptualization of the pan-Canaanite *ḥerem* to the time of Josiah because it seems consistent with zealously nationalistic, expansionistic, and religious impulses that they perceive in his reign.[50] On literary grounds, however, the connection between these passages and Dtr's account of Josiah in 2 Kings is actually quite weak. Not only does Josiah fail to undertake any program of wholesale slaughter that resembles the *ḥerem*, but not even the language of cultic reform employed in Deuteronomy 7 and 12 corresponds with the description of Josiah's purgation of cultic objects. On the whole, Josiah's elimination of cultic objects and personnel is described with much more specific language, and where particular objects correspond between 2 Kings 23 and Deuteronomy 7 and 12, the destructions are phrased differently. For example, the 2 Kings 23 account demonstrates a concern with the *bāmâ* (e.g., 23:15) that is common in Samuel-Kings, but apart from the poem in Deuteronomy 32–33, it is entirely absent from both Deuteronomy and Joshua. Likewise, while the verb gd^c is used in Deuteronomy 7 and 12 to describe the felling of cult objects (ʾăšêrîm in 7:5 and pĕsîlê ʾĕlōhîm in 12:3), this verb is nowhere to be found in the account of Josiah. Instead, the verb krt is used of the cutting down of ʾăšêrîm in 2 Kings 23:14, a term that never occurs as a verb of cultic destruction in Deuteronomy. All this is to say that the language of Deuteronomy and 2 Kings is not closely intertwined on the subject of cultic purgation, much less as regards the ḥerem.

Furthermore, the most distinctive uses of ḥerem language in the Dtr corpus, those that seem to envision a comprehensive annihilation of the inhabitants of Canaan as Israel inherits the land, do not sit entirely easily in their contexts. It is easy, and perhaps even an improvement, to extract the language of ḥerem from Deuteronomy 7:2, where it awkwardly interposes itself into the commands about how Israel might coexist but not mix with the—presumably living—Canaanite peoples. Deuteronomy 20:15–18 could be removed with little damage to the laws of warfare, and even Sihon and Og are fully conquered in 2:34 and 3:6 with the statements about the ḥerem excised from their accounts. Similarly, the summaries in Joshua 10–11 are phrased in a highly formulaic way that points back to their fulfillment of the ḥerem as total annihilation of the nearby nations of Canaan, as expressed in Deuteronomy 7:2 and 20:17.[51] The summary statements of regional conquest in Joshua 10:40 and 11:14 and the conquest of the particularly important city of Hazor in 11:11 ("the head of all these kingdoms") adopt the distinctive phrase "everything that breathes" (kol-nĕšāmâ) employed by Deuteronomy 20:16,[52] pointing to a textual connection between the commands in Deuteronomy and their fulfillment in Joshua. The stereotyped phrasing and self-referential, self-contained nature of these passages raise the suspicion that they do not belong to the earliest stratum of the works we know as Deuteronomy and DtrH. I would argue that evidence offered by the text is best explained by J. Levenson's theory about the secondary interpolation of what he designates as the "Book of the Torah" or "Dtn," consisting of Deuteronomy 4:44–28:68, into Deuteronomy by an exilic hand.[53] In his reading, the Deuteronomistic code of law becomes part of the book of Deuteronomy and of DtrH as a whole not under the looming aegis of Josiah, but by the hand of an exilic redactor. Such an understanding revolutionizes our vision of the purpose of this text and its socio-political context. As Levenson expresses it, "Dtn is introduced not as the program gloriously realized by royal fiat, but as a bill of indictment against a sinning nation prosecuted by a God who calls on heaven and earth to witness against them (Deut 4:25ff., 30:19ff., 31:28ff.). In its present position, Dtn is a cause not for self-congratulation, but for self-reproach."[54] Read in such a context, I would argue, the *ḥerem* commands and their obedient fulfillment take on a radically different meaning from the one they would have as the decrees of a religiously zealous monarch with the power of state behind his commands.

As a result, we must begin with the foundational recognition that the blanket *ḥerem* applied to the Canaanites originates as a *literary motif*. Israel did not slaughter any actual Canaanites in this manner, both because there were no Canaanite nations to slaughter at the time of writing[55] *and* because that is simply not the point of the metaphor, as we will see below. As discussed in the preceding section on the historical development of the concept of the *ḥerem*, the idea of a generalized commitment to *ḥerem* in Israel's taking of the land appears to be an *innovation* of the later Deuteronomistic redactors of DtrH. That is to say, this language is not an existing primitivism that they struggle to modify humanely and interpret theologically.[56] Instead, the Deuteronomistic writers *choose to adopt* the past practice of the spontaneous *ḥerem* vow for the literary purpose of depicting the degree of devotion to YHWH and separation from idolaters and idolatry which they hold as the ideal for their contemporaries. I would suggest, then, that what we witness here is both a metaphorization of the language of *ḥerem*, and the narrative reactivation and reactualization of that language.[57]

Understood in this way, the Dtr adoption of the language of *ḥerem* could be understood as a development similar to the revival of the image of YHWH as warrior in later biblical texts, as observed by F. M. Cross,[58] and the transformation of the ideal of the dedication of the firstborn son reflected in Judaism and Christianity, as described by

Levenson.[59] Both the totality of devotion required by the traditional *ḥerem* vow and the degree of destruction it entailed are subsumed within a double-edged metaphor of the need for Israel's obedience and the threat of its disobedience. This literary reactivation of the *ḥerem* is aimed neither at non-Israelites nor at "outsiders" within Israel, but at the whole people chosen by YHWH who have strayed from Him and suffered for it. Actual execution of the *ḥerem* in relation to Canaanite neighbors is situated in the past, which—against the protestations of some scholars[60]—is entirely relevant to the mitigation of the practice in relation to non-Israelites.[61] The so-called seven nations of Canaan do not correspond to national entities in Dtr²'s own historical situation, but instead serve as symbols of social and cultic temptations that threaten to distract Israel from its allegiance to YHWH, bringing us back to the metaphorical dimension of Dtr's use of *ḥerem* terms.[62] Nor can the *ḥerem* texts, read in context, credibly be interpreted as a paradigm for international relations in the exile, despite what some scholars argue,[63] since Deuteronomy explicitly limits the *ḥerem* to the nations in the land that YHWH has given Israel as its inheritance.[64]

Instead, the *ḥerem* of the Canaanites is a "myth" of the truest sort, at once holding up to Israel a mirror of its own sin and recalling its mandate for obedience, reminding Israel simultaneously of the punishment meted out for idolatry and of its own susceptibility to straying toward other gods. The Dtr redactors craft the *ḥerem* motif in order to let the cultic sins and punishment of the Canaanites serve as a mirror of Israel's own experience of YHWH's wrath resulting from its idolatry. Ironically—and tellingly—it seems that in Dtr's present situation only the *ḥerem* commands in Deuteronomy 13 with regard to idolatrous *Israelites* could conceivably be implemented in a practical way.[65] The literary motif of the *ḥerem* of the Canaanites originates in a situation in which Israel finds *itself*, rather than enemy nations, bearing the brunt of YHWH's wrath. Thus, while scholars often treat the *ḥerem* texts as tools of imperialism, oppression, or coercion,[66] it seems to me far more probable that a redactor of DtrH crafted the motif of the comprehensive *ḥerem* based upon the experience of exile. Israel's own experience of expulsion from the land and of YHWH's opposition toward itself serve as the model for describing the *ḥerem* of the Canaanites and warning against the dire threat of idolatry. Properly understood, these texts are a matter of life and death not for the Canaanites or any "foreign" peoples, but for Israel.

Seen in this light, Israel's account of its mandate to supplant the Canaanites functions neither as the "power fantasy" of a small but resurgent Judah under Josiah's rule, nor as the "revenge fantasy" of a powerless people in exile under foreign rule. Instead, Dtr² holds up the *ḥerem* as a mirror in which Israel may see its own sins of idolatry, offering in Israel's driving out of the Canaanites, their subjection to the *ḥerem*, and the seizure of their land a retrospective "foreshadowing" of Israel's own dispossession and dispersion by the Babylonians. As a result, the *ḥerem* motif is crafted not so much to make the point that Canaanites are wicked—the message that modern readers often mistakenly come away with—but rather to convey that the idolatrous wickedness of Israel is just as much subject to YHWH's wrath as the idolatrous wickedness of the Canaanites.[67]

Deuteronomy's use of the motif alone might not provide persuasive support for this understanding of the *ḥerem*. Further bolstering this interpretation, however, is Deuteronomy's further exposition in chapters 7–9 of the "basic" formulation of the *ḥerem* found in chapter 7. In these chapters, Deuteronomy interweaves commendations toward obedience with sharp reminders of Israel's own fallibility and susceptibility to idolatry, culminating in Deuteronomy 9 with the account of Israel's sin with the golden calf. Again and again, the text undercuts any possible assertion of Israel's own worthiness, qualifications, or even ability to occupy the land of Canaan. The text directly and unabashedly makes the point that YHWH's choice of Israel as the agent of Canaan's punishment and heir of the land has nothing to do with Israel's own superior virtue (9:4–6), size (7:7), or strength (7:17, 8:17). Instead, Israel's supplanting of Canaan rests solely upon YHWH's fulfillment of His promise to the ancestors (Deut 9:5).

This undercutting of a nation's belief in its own choice and ability to conquer resembles the view of Israel's punishment by means of Assyria offered in Isaiah 10:5–19. Here, Assyria serves as the "rod" of

YHWH's wrath, acting not on its own initiative or power but as nothing more than a tool of YHWH for punishment (Isa 10:5, 15). Just as Deuteronomy admonishes Israel against believing that its own qualifications bring about its success, the speaker in Isaiah warns that the Assyrian ruler will in due time experience the consequences for his arrogant belief in his own power and initiative (Isa 10:12–19). Ultimately, it is YHWH who chooses nations to enact His will, and the nation that punishes is no more entitled to boast than the nation that is conquered. In addition, the nation that punishes is just as susceptible to being punished in turn, should it fail to acknowledge YHWH's power—even Israel itself. It is to this end that Deuteronomy intertwines commands regarding Israel's purgation of idolatry from the land with stark reminders of Israel's own rebellious tendencies and its ongoing need for awareness of YHWH's provision. Even as conqueror of Canaan, Israel paradoxically must carry out its role with humility rather than with triumphalism, painfully aware of the role that its own fallibility plays in the need for Canaan's supplanting.[68]

The Ḥerem in the Context of Ancient Israel

As we have seen, the ḥerem makes no sense when viewed through an Enlightenment lens of humanistic ethics and reason. Nor is it properly understood in terms of twentieth-century experiences of genocide driven by religious or ethnic intolerance, or as the bloodthirsty imaginings of a junto of religious fanatics. Rather, the extremity and enormity of the ḥerem injunctions correspond to the extremity of Israel's situation as a people that has fallen under YHWH's wrath, and therefore bear a message for Israel itself: the extremity and totality with which the idolatrous inhabitants of Canaan are to be eradicated is the same degree of force with which YHWH strikes Israel because it failed to serve Him alone. Only by giving its full and undivided allegiance to YHWH and shunning idolatrous ways, as YHWH has commanded, can Israel once again hope to experience YHWH's blessings in the land. None of this does, in fact, make sense in a generally understandable, commonly shared, Enlightened modern parlance. Quite the opposite, this language is *particular* language, a conversation among "insiders" that assumes the existence of "outsiders." It is, in addition, a conversation rife with *premodern* ideas about the world and a particular people's place in it. Although it makes little sense within the bounds of the modern liberal imagination, it would have made a great deal of sense to Israel, who would have understood how the parlance of *ḥerem*, employing a familiar concept in a new way, expressed Israel's need for exclusive allegiance to YHWH.

How Gibeon Escaped the *Ḥerem*

Only after the fact, as in the successful conquest of Jericho following the oath to Rahab, does YHWH's implicit approval of Israel's rectification of its hasty error become evident. In the next chapter, the Gibeonites call upon their allies, the Israelites, to defend them against a Canaanite coalition; not only does Israel come to their aid, but YHWH Himself declares that He has already given the enemies of Gibeon into Israel's hand (Josh 10:8). By this action, He seems to give His approval to Israel's preservation of the Gibeonites' lives and to reinforce this by saving them Himself, through Israel, a second time.[69] What began as a story of deception ends as a story of mercy demonstrated by both Israel and YHWH.

In conclusion, Israel demonstrates a faithfulness to YHWH that is not infallible but that acknowledges and reconciles transgression even when it fails to act rightly. Once again, as in the case of Achan, Israel's leaders demonstrate faithfulness in seeking to restore Israel's right standing before YHWH by proposing a resolution to the treaty-making that acknowledges Israel's own role in the matter. This outcome of the story places a priority on keeping a treaty made before YHWH, giving it precedence even over the execution of the theoretically unilateral command of *ḥerem*—an outcome similar to that of the oath made to Rahab. Joshua's modification of the sentence shifts the Gibeonites' service where it is ultimately due: to YHWH, as both deity and suzerain, whom neither Israel nor Gibeon properly recognized in the making of the treaty. Yet both peoples meet with YHWH's mercy rather than destruction, all because Israel extends to treacherous Gibeon a mercy similar to what it has itself repeatedly experienced from YHWH.

The Transjordanian Altar: Apostasy or Testimony?

A Backdrop of Faithfulness

When the tribes of Israel part after dividing the land, dispersing to occupy their own territories, the narrative conveys a certain sense of closure—and relief. The return of the Transjordanian tribes to their allotments across the river seems to indicate that, in spite of the text's intimations that Israel has not fully completed its task of receiving the land, a satisfactory degree of occupation has been achieved for the present at least.[70] The text itself acknowledges a significant shift from the stage of conquest to the era of settlement by the sweeping statement of 21:43–45: "Thus the Lord gave to Israel all the land that He had sworn to give to their ancestors, and they subdued it and dwelt in it. The Lord gave rest to them all around according to all that He had sworn to their ancestors, and no one stood against them from all their enemies; all of their enemies the Lord delivered into their hand. Not a thing went unfulfilled from the entire good word that the Lord spoke to the house of Israel; everything came to pass." A number of commentators take this statement as a heavily ironic rather than sincere statement of what occurred in Israel's taking of the land, given the incomplete settlement portrayed in the book.[71] In my view, however, the structure of the story itself does not support this reading. The narrative treats this moment as a satisfactory end to the era of active conquest,[72] following it with the return of the Transjordanian tribes to their allotted territory. Joshua 1 has already prepared the reader to treat their departure as a signal that marks a shift from the era of "settlement" into an era of "settledness," since it will not occur until the Cisjordanian territorial acquisition is complete.

The parting of ways between Israel and Israel at the beginning of chapter 22 marks the end of the period of conquest partly by taking us back to the first chapter of the book. There, while all Israel was still encamped on the east bank of the Jordan, the Transjordanian tribes made their promise to Joshua that they would fight alongside their kinsmen until they had taken possession of the land west of the Jordan (Josh 1:12–18). Now the text indicates that they have fulfilled their word, just as YHWH has fulfilled His.

Ironically, but forebodingly, the story of the dispute over the Transjordanian altar follows like a dark shadow cast before this wide-ranging, inspiring conclusion. New challenges are beginning even as the old ones are ending. The absence of opposition more pointedly brings into focus what may ultimately pose the greatest threat to Israel's survival: Israel's own danger to itself. On the heels of "rest on every side" from the enemies who had opposed Israel's reception of its inheritance (21:44) comes a reminder of the truth that Israel's fate is never completely settled; YHWH's plans for Israel do not end at a fixed point but continue to unfold in the context of the ongoing relationship between God and people. Thus, even with the long-awaited fulfillment of the promise of land to the ancestors (21:43, 45), Israel may fail to serve YHWH by violating His commandments and refusing to acknowledge His sole sovereignty, thereby bringing upon itself YHWH's wrath and its own destruction (24:19–20). Unlike the temptation toward Canaanite worship practices, this danger cannot be eradicated by the defeat of non-Israelite enemies and secure dwelling in the promised land. Israel must vigilantly and persistently practice YHWH's commandments and continue in the proper worship of Him alone, as summarized by Joshua's parting words to the Transjordanian tribes in 22:5. Israel's task of claiming its inheritance may be finished, but its most challenging work has just begun.

While the earlier stories in the book of Joshua have already foreshadowed the danger of Israel's undermining YHWH's efforts on its behalf,[73] this danger reaches its climax in this final narrative of the settlement as Israel, freed from external opposition, threatens to divide and conquer itself. The cause for this internal tension is a crisis of obedience—a hermeneutical dilemma surrounding an altar built by the body of eastern tribes as they return to their land across the Jordan.[74] The story frames the question from the perspective of the western tribes, who, like the reader, are not privy to the eastern tribes' rationale in building the altar—namely, is the building of this altar by the Transjordanians an act of apostasy?[75] If the altar in fact turns out to be an expression of rebellion against YHWH, it threatens to destroy the unity of the newly settled people of YHWH, instigating division and strife within just as rest from external forces at last has become possible.[76] This raises the question of the story's purpose: why does the text place this incident at a point at which it threatens to disrupt the idyllic picture of Israelite unity and success so recently presented? Only a consideration of the source of the story in connection with the purpose of its inclusion in the book will satisfactorily answer this question.

Whose Story Is Joshua 22?

An analysis of the source history of the altar episode in Joshua 22 and its place within the development of the book poses some challenges. To begin with, the story lies within a block of material that scholars frequently exclude from the first edition of DtrH, observing the use of nearly identical phrasing in 13:1a and 23:1b as a means of bracketing the material in between.[77] While this resumption could be used as a literary device to frame Dtr's incorporation of a block of existing material, it is more commonly understood as indicating the interpolation of material added after the initial version of DtrH had already taken shape. Further complicating matters of attribution, the story contains some vocabulary typical of Dtr and some vocabulary more characteristic of P, as well as thematic elements such as centralized worship that conceivably could be attributed to either one.[78] Scholars generally attribute the first few verses containing Joshua's dismissal of the Transjordanian tribes to Dtr (21:1–8), then allot the altar story itself to P (vv. 9–34);[79] the distribution of P and Dtr vocabulary, though, does not line up so neatly with this division.

The story's echoes of other biblical material raise yet more questions instead of providing answers. Its reference to Achan is easy enough to explain, but determining the source of the writer's knowledge of the Baal Peor incident poses more of a challenge. Does the compiler of Joshua 22 know the text of Numbers 25, or only a legend of Phinehas as it has been told to him? Neither Joshua 22 nor Numbers 25 provides firm enough evidence to answer this question with certainty. Similar problems arise in determining whether distinctive phrases that this story shares with others demonstrate the writer's intent to evoke those other texts, or whether the shared language stems from a similarity of subject matter or the infrequent textual preservation of a familiar Hebrew phrase. For example, the phrase "You have no portion in YHWH," feared by the Transjordanian tribes, could be read as anticipating the phrase "no share in *David*" spoken in rebellion against Judahite leadership in 2 Samuel 20:1 and 1 Kings 12:16.[80] In light of this similarity, a north-south resonance might be found in the east-west tribal conflict depicted in Joshua 22, and the story's origin and purpose determined on this basis. On the other hand, the story also bears a striking resemblance on a number of levels to Laban's and Jacob's construction of the mound they call "witness" in Genesis 31.[81] Not only the name of the mound, but the position of both episodes before the crossing of a river into one's home territory, as well as the conceptualization of monuments as a sign between human parties witnessed by a divine enforcer, suggest some connection between the two. Neither of these comparisons, though, establishes a strong enough connection either verbally or thematically between Joshua 22 and the texts compared to it, leaving their relationship—and the text's "source affiliation"—unclear.

I would argue that the most likely scenario of the story's history is as follows. Inclusion of this story in a version of DtrH penned during the reign of Josiah seems unlikely, considering Josiah's vigorous destruction of illicit southern and northern altars; this conciliatory piece with its permission to maintain a noncentral altar grates against his centralizing reforms, even with the guarantee of disuse. The tone of the story does not bear the mark of a king who desecrates unauthorized cult sites with human bones, nor does it point to Judah unified under a monarch ruling over a single contiguous territory. Instead, it speaks to a time when geographical dispersion has broken Israel apart, when this distance threatens to create a rift between those west of the Jordan and those east of it.

In that context, I would analyze the story's process of incorporation as follows: An old altar story transmitted and reworked in priestly circles[82] is incorporated by Dtr[2] in the exile[83] to serve as a persuasive piece. In this new context, both the story's suggestions of P origins and the presence of Phinehas and his authoritative role point more to the story's *function* and *address* as adopted by Dtr[2] than to its origins. Dtr[2] adopts this story as a parable for priestly groups who have begun the renewal of postexilic Jewish worship in Jerusalem. Through the depiction in the story of the negotiations between the western and eastern tribes over the altar, Dtr[2] presents a model for these priests, urging them to match their zeal to maintain the purity of worship with equal efforts to maintain religious ties with those who have no access to the Jerusalem cult. Instead of responding with suspicion to the worship practices of those still in exile, Dtr[2] offers a model for carefully and deliberately investigating and communicating about the motives and meaning of the practices that these Jews east of the Jordan engage in. In addition, he prefaces the story with a speech by Joshua, evoking the positive evaluation of the Transjordanian tribes maintained throughout the book and imbuing them with a history of faithfulness that casts their construction of the altar in a favorable light.

This explanation of the story's purpose would account for both its P and Dtr elements, as well as the retention of "P language" in a story incorporated by a Dtr redactor. Furthermore, integration by Dtr[2] rather than a P redactor would explain its comfortable fit with the themes already woven throughout the book.[84] With this understanding of the story's background and incorporation into the book of Joshua in view, we now turn to an analysis of how the story communicates its message in its present context.[85]

The Mechanics of the Altar Story

The controversial subject matter and complex composition make this story rich with interpretive possibilities and abounding in questions clamoring to be answered. In light of the theory presented above, however, three less adequately explored features of the story take on particular importance. First, the initial eight verses of the chapter, often left aside as extraneous to the main action, must be recognized as background for the reading of the dispute that follows in the present form of the text, regardless of their source derivation. These verses assert the eastern tribes' faithfulness from the start, and it is the recognition of this by the western tribes that ultimately enables the debate's—and the story's—resolution. Second, the figure of Phinehas, familiar from his rectification of cultic violations in Numbers 25 and their sequel in Numbers 31, plays a distinctive role as the leader of the commission sent by the western tribes. Together, his previous record of militant zeal for the purity of YHWH's cult and his priestly lineage invest his affirmation of the legitimacy of the altar alongside the western tribes with authority. Third, the description of the altar by the western tribes as a *tabnît*, distancing it from the concept of a functioning sacrificial altar and from itself serving as a representation of the divine presence, creates a space for the meaningful construction of altars outside the central cult. In this way, the tensions within Israel that this altar creates and the questions it raises with regard to Israel's faithfulness in worship are framed in such a way that their telling addresses the needs and concerns of both priestly and lay readers dispersed by exile.

The Transjordanians' History of Faithfulness

Some commentators have observed that the story of the altar dispute offers readers little orientation as to where to place their sympathies.[86] No explanation of the altar from the perspective of its builders is provided in the text at the time of its building in Joshua 22:10; the first interpretation that the reader encounters, in the following verse, is the snap judgment of the western tribes that their kinsmen have apostatized. Without any knowledge of the builders' own explanation, readers are left to assess the true meaning of the altar as the dispute evolves between the eastern and western tribes, evaluating motives and arguments alongside the participants as the story unfolds.

To some extent, this perception is accurate. Especially in comparison with the front-loaded and detailed notice of Achan's crime in the Jericho account—where the narrative states explicitly that a crime was committed, who committed it, and what resulted (Josh 7:1)—readers are left quite in the dark as to what moral judgment they should make on the central action of the story. The text withholds from the reader any special knowledge that would enable a decisive interpretation of the altar before Israel itself has reached a conclusion, thereby drawing the reader into the dispute.

As is typical of biblical narrative, though, the situation is in fact more nuanced than this. Reticence is widely recognized as part of the Bible's narrative's art,[87] such that part of the reader's task in dealing with the text's subtler mechanics is to recognize the value of the information that the reader *is* given rather than ruing what is left unsaid. Here, the reader's advantage lies in having "overheard" Joshua's speech to the Transjordanian tribes.[88] This speech provides information useful to the reader in the debate that follows, in that, first, it affirms the Transjordanians' faithfulness up to this point, and second, it affirms the divine legitimation of their habitation of the land east of the Jordan. Joshua begins by lauding the Transjordanian tribes' faithfulness in fulfilling the commands of both Joshua and Moses in a general sense (22:1–2), and more specifically, by engaging in warfare on behalf of the Cisjordanian tribes as they had promised (22:3). Joshua's observation that the Transjordanian tribes have enabled their kin to have "rest" in their own allotted territory (v. 4) gives their obedience even greater significance by interpreting it as participation in the fulfillment of YHWH's promises to Israel.[89] Notably, both of Joshua's central points of commendation involve their loyalty to their fellow Israelites (vv. 3–4). Joshua concludes his praise of the eastern tribes by urging carefulness about continued obedience to the Lord in verse 5. As it turns out, this verse raises a fear that will manifest itself in the exchange that ensues between the two clusters of tribes divided by the Jordan River: the fear that geographical separation will result in separation from YHWH. For the time being, this fear is held at bay; within the context of the speech, this exhortation primarily functions to encourage the eastern tribes to continue on the path they have thus far chosen—to keep up the good work, so to speak.

In addition to lauding these acts of faithfulness rendered to their fellow Israelites, Joshua's speech not only affirms but *emphasizes* the legitimacy of the Transjordanians' return to their own land across the Jordan. Contrary to the distinction between Transjordan and "YHWH's land" which will characterize the views of the western tribes in the ensuing narrative,[90] the occupation of the land east of the Jordan is thoroughly justified by the invocation of all key authorities: Joshua, Moses, and YHWH. Once in Joshua's speech and once in the narrator's own voice, the appropriateness of the occupation of the land east of the Jordan is reiterated. In Joshua 22:4 the eastern territory is designated as "the land that Moses the servant of the Lord gave you on the other side of the Jordan," setting a firm authority behind their occupation of this territory, grounded in Moses' actions under the authority of YHWH. Further reinforcing this point, the narrator informs us in 22:9 that the eastern tribes returned to "their own land, which they had acquired in accordance with the command of the Lord through Moses." The text leaves no doubt that both YHWH and Moses have authorized the eastern tribes to inherit this land (Num 32), reiterating that this move to the far bank of the Jordan is an act of obedience, constituting neither retrogression nor desertion.

Up to this point, the opening verses of chapter 22 have subtly prepared the reader for the report in verse 10 that on their way home, the Transjordanians build an altar. At this point in the story, the reader learns only two things about the altar: that it is located near the Jordan River (vv. 10–11),[91] and that it is described as *gādôl lĕmarʾeh* (v. 10).[92] No comment is made at this point about whether it is built in the Israelite manner or in a pagan style; whether its purpose is the worship of YHWH or the service of other gods. Instead of further information about the altar itself, the text offers the reader only a clear view of the subjective reaction of the western tribes, who, upon hearing of the altar, immediately prepare to go to war against their kinsmen.

As it turns out, this placement of the altar-building notice is quite strategic. Immediately preceding the notice, the reader witnesses Joshua's accolades and parting words to the eastern tribes; immediately after the notice, the reader finds the Cisjordanians nearly instantaneously deciding to go to war upon the clear presupposition that the altar's construction indicates apostasy. By framing the notice in this way, the text ingeniously offers two possible contexts in which to interpret the building of the altar: that is, it can be understood either in light of the Transjordanians' long record of faithfulness, as recounted in Joshua 22:1–9, or in accord with the western tribes' swift conclusion that their brothers have strayed into improper worship (v. 11).

If read in light of what precedes, this juxtaposition of texts suggests the possibility that the building of the altar can be understood as entirely consistent with the manner in which the Transjordanians have conducted themselves up to this point. From this perspective, the faithfulness of the Transjordanians in earlier matters accords with their action in this matter, suggesting that they are acting now in good faith just as the reader knows—through Joshua's speech in 22:1–8—that they have in the past.

If the reader looks instead to the Cisjordanians' response for the interpretation of the altar's construction, this action comes as a shock, an appalling abandonment of YHWH by the Transjordanians at the first opportunity. As a result, the western tribes resolve to respond to this transgression with equal speed, with the consequences of Achan's crime perhaps still jarringly fresh in their memory. The text does not make clear whether the western tribes were present to serve as audience for Joshua's words extolling the faithfulness of the Transjordanians in 22:1–8. In any case, the Cisjordanians should be aware of this history precisely as the beneficiaries of the eastern tribes' faithfulness therein described—it was for their sake that the Transjordanian tribes crossed the Jordan, away from their homes and families, in the first place. Although the Cisjordanian tribes have been witnesses to the eastern tribes' history of faithfulness, they are apparently forgetful ones. As for readers, however, the text lets them weigh both the Transjordanians' history and the Cisjordanians' response in the process of forming an opinion about the altar.

After this turning point, at which two interpretive possibilities regarding the meaning of the altar hang suspended for a moment, the text plunges ahead into the western tribes' suspicions. As the attacking group, they have the first say. Yet on the western side of the Jordan, one figure is surprisingly silent: Joshua himself, who so recently offered the commendations that could best come to the defense of the eastern tribes. Joshua's role in this narrative—or more prominently, his absence after the opening speech of the chapter—adds to its interest. In a manner that recalls the divine silence throughout the Gibeonite episode, here neither the Lord nor Joshua, His appointed leader, offers a word of guidance or adjudication.[93] As in the case of the Gibeonite dilemma, Israel must rely on previously spoken words to assess and resolve the situation in which it finds itself. No authoritative word arrives to intervene in the debate; everything must be worked out between the human parties by means of argument.

The Roles of Authority and Debate

Yet the western tribes are not without a leader. A figure legendary for his zeal for the Lord, "Phinehas, son of Eleazar the priest" (Josh 22:13), mysteriously appears for the first time in the book to serve as the chief commissioner of the Israelite investigative committee. Although the text offers no explicit rationale, it is clear that his leadership in this narrative recalls his legendary role in the Baal of Peor incident in Numbers 25, which is referred to later in the chapter (Josh 22:17) as an example of Israelite apostasy.[94] In that incident, his decisive and timely action halted the progress of the plague that had struck the Israelites as punishment for their sexual and cultic activities with Moabite women. As B. Organ puts it, "Phinehas is established in this, his first active appearance, as the faithful priest who can be counted on to defend the proper worship of YHWH."[95] This incident is directly invoked in the debate over the altar as a comparative example from the past of how Israel will corporately pay for its cultic misdeeds (22:17).[96] Phinehas's selection as ambassador points to the Israelites' concern that this case have a similar outcome—that it will require the intervention of a man so "zealous for the honor of his God" (Num 25:13) that he will not hesitate to slay even fellow Israelites, if necessary.

In the course of the debate over the altar, Phinehas makes no independent verbal contribution; he speaks only as part of the chorus composed of the members of the western delegation (Josh 22:15–20). Based on his two previous appearances in Numbers, this suits his character as a man of action, not words—a fact that itself constitutes a commentary on the situation he is sent to deal with in Joshua 22. When he finally speaks alone at the end of the discussion in Joshua 22:31, it is the first time he has spoken a solo part in any of his appearances. Notably, it is with the purpose of offering the concluding—and conclusive—verdict that the eastern tribes' response shows the presence of the Lord with all those gathered (22:31).[97] Instead of meting out punishment, he reverses the situation, declaring that the Transjordanians' explanation has forestalled YHWH's retribution against the *Israelites* (apparently referring to the western tribes here) by arresting their misplaced zeal (Josh 22:31). In what might come as a stunning change to readers familiar with his previous exploits, Phinehas at last breaks his silence, finding conciliatory words rather than military action to be his most appropriate contribution to this cultic debate. We would not expect the hero who speared a copulating Israelite man and Moabite woman in one motion to be hesitant about resorting to violence. That Phinehas is ultimately convinced by the Transjordanians' argument functions to lend it substantial credibility for priestly readers, revealing his main function in the story as used by Dtr². While both Phinehas and the western tribes are satisfied with the argument presented by the Transjordanians,[98] Phinehas fulfills a vital role by stepping in to deliver the only individual authoritative word addressed to the situation, declaring to the eastern tribes, "Today we know that YHWH is in our midst, because you have not rebelled against YHWH with this rebellious act; furthermore, you have rescued the children of Israel from the hand of YHWH" (Josh 22:31). His statement, even as it represents the consensus of the western tribes as a whole, has behind it the weightiness of his qualifications as "Phinehas the son of Eleazar, the priest" (v. 31a), validating their response and sealing the dispute.

With this taciturn leader at the head of the western tribes, the debate itself is carried out on relatively equal ground between the two groups of Israelites from either side of the Jordan. That is to say, no authoritative word dominates the argument or tips the balance of power toward one interpretation or the other as each of the two sides presents its case. As stated above, the reader's understanding of the situation must rely upon—and, significantly, the western tribes' understanding largely *fails* to rely upon—previous authoritative speech, none of which is directly appealed to in the situation. Rather, the western tribes' argument invokes the history of the effects of apostasy in Israel (see 22:17, 20) as parallel to the Transjordanians' action, portraying the altar-building as an act by which the eastern tribes *actively seek to separate themselves* from worship of YHWH. In so doing, the Cisjordanian tribes omit another more immediately relevant piece of evidence from Israel's history, exhibit A presented by Dtr² at the beginning of Joshua 22: the record of faithfulness attributed to the eastern tribes by Joshua (22:1-8).⁹⁹ The Transjordanian tribes' own rhetoric, on the other hand, rightly assumes that history of faithfulness, but demonstrates a corresponding mistrust of their western brethren as they cite their concern about *involuntary exclusion* from YHWH's cult in the future as the cause for their altar building (22:27-28). In fact, the eastern tribes' worst fears have already been rhetorically realized because of the very symbol that was intended to forestall such an outcome, as the Cisjordanians functionally sequester the name "children of Israel" for themselves as they gather against their eastern kin (22:11-14).¹⁰⁰ Thus, the altar paradoxically embodies the eastern tribes' fear that geographical distance will lead to their disinheritance from worship of YHWH, and ignites the western tribes' fear that geographical distance will lead to voluntary separation from worship of YHWH—transforming both parties' concern for unity into a cause for division.

Where does the deliberate inclusion in this story of the *process* of Israel's debate over the altar fit into what Dtr hopes to convey to the priestly circles that he addresses by this text? At first, the story's involved and lengthy exchange that results in the justification of a peculiarly inoperative altar might appear to be an argument in favor of the construction of cult objects outside the central cult. The framing of the debate in terms of the initial concern of apostasy met with acceptable explanations, including an affirmation of the central YHWHistic cult, could suggest this—that Dtr[2] supports the use of YHWHistic cult replicas as "icons" of YHWH, symbols of YHWH's presence outside of the central cult site.

A close reading shows, however, that the story never actually portrays the *altar itself* as a symbol of YHWH's presence for the Transjordanians. Significantly, the divine presence is intentionally affirmed in the speech of Phinehas as exhibited by the demonstrated *faithfulness* of the Transjordanians (v. 31). As for the altar, it is instead framed as a "witness" to the eastern tribes' permanent and valid right to participation in the western-centered YHWHistic cult (vv. 27–28). In short, it serves as a symbol of Israel's *unity* under YHWH despite geographical separation—a timely issue at the moment of Israel's dispersal to its territorial allotments after its unified action throughout the book.

The Meaning of *Tabnît*

The elucidation of the altar's meaning in this regard is to be sought in its description as a *tabnît* of YHWH's sacrificial altar (v. 28). *Tabnît* has neither unequivocally positive nor negative connotations in the Hebrew Bible.[101] The word can denote both the divinely bestowed pattern for the tabernacle (Ex 29:9, 40) and the illicit making of images (Deut 4:16–18). Sometimes it is used to form literary analogies,[102] but more frequently, though not exclusively, it occurs in relation to cultic objects. Its main sense is that of a representation, whether of a creature or artifact, that either precedes the existence of a reality as a plan or pattern for its making, or represents and replicates a reality already in existence.[103] Understood in this way, a *tabnît* of YHWH's altar points not to YHWH's presence itself, but to another *altar* that precedes it— the functioning, sacrificial altar of the Israelite cult. As an icon, it is a second-order symbol that points to a cult object, which in turn points to the deity served. To put it differently, this "replica" exercises its symbolism on a horizontal plane; it points to another earthly reality that itself operates on a vertical plane, functioning in Israel's worship of its God. According to the eastern tribes, then, this "replica" serves as a reminder that the worship that takes place at the "real" altar of YHWH west of the Jordan is the domain of the western and eastern tribes alike—that YHWH is God on both sides of the Jordan (v. 34). Thus, the Transjordanians' monumental altar is allowed to stand as a witness that these eastern tribes will never be denied their place among YHWH's elect who are privileged to serve Him.

D$_{tr^2}$'s purpose for recounting this story to later Israel seems to arise most naturally from the divinely unarbitrated cultic dispute laid out in the text, providing guidance for Israel's use of this text in its ongoing life as a community. The story illustrates the negotiation of a cultic dispute between two groups of Israelites without the benefit of a civil leader or a divine word spoken directly to the situation. Instead, Phinehas, a legendary priestly figure, appears as the leader of the "prosecuting party"; in this capacity, though, he offers a verdict that does not itself decide the situation, but rather validates and lends its authority to the group's decision. By so doing, the story gives priestly weight to the conclusion reached and the process of negotiation used to achieve it. Nonetheless, the decision that is made depends, in the end, upon mutual trust among all Israel, since the western tribes have only their kinsmen's word on which to base their decision. The outcome of the story obliquely directs the reader back to the faithful record of the "defending" party cited by Joshua (22:1–8) as an accurate reflection of the eastern tribes' motives in building the altar. Thus, the redactor who incorporates this story commends to his audience a careful process of listening and discussion to evaluate the validity of the worship practices of Jews who live far from Jerusalem rather than a hasty response of censure and disassociation.

It is this tenuous but satisfactory explanation that somehow makes the story and bears its central theme. Against the claims of some commentators, the story treats the Transjordanians' vigorous assertions of the nonsacrificial character of the altar as true representations of their intentions.[104] Neither readers nor the Cisjordanian tribes can discern anything more than this; neither characters within the story nor readers of it have access to anything besides the eastern tribes' words, set against their past actions, on which to base their conclusions. As the text presents the situation, this evidence—the only evidence we have—is enough.

Phinehas's concord with their satisfaction at the Transjordanians' answer underscores the appropriateness of this trust. At the same time, it reflects a caution with regard to recourse to violence as a solution to inner-Israelite conflicts. Even Phinehas, who has not hesitated to use violence as the tool of cultic zeal in the past, is content to confine himself to words here. Although the consequences of covenant transgression are indeed grave, as Achan's story has shown, this story points to the need for trust and communication to balance out the equally necessary caution and prompt rectification of sins committed within Israel. In a final reversal, the violence that was to be enacted on the basis of zeal for YHWH and a concern for Israelite unity is shown to have been, in this case, a sin that might have destroyed Israel (Josh 22:31).

Perhaps most importantly, the story decisively conveys that Israel divided by a river need not be Israel separated from YHWH or divided within itself. As a stone monument built on the banks of the Jordan at the moment of crossing, this altar erected by the eastern tribes recalls the memorial raised by the twelve tribes together in Joshua 4 as they first entered the land.[105] This monument recalled that there, for a little while, YHWH had not let a river stand in the way of His promises; for a brief time, the two banks were joined by dry land and the river posed no barrier to Israel (4:7–8 and 22–23). In this "back-crossing" of the Jordan, the building of the altar by the Transjordanians recalls the memorial stones erected upon Israel's entry into the land. Before YHWH's ark, the sign of His presence, the waters receded; by this action, YHWH temporarily fused the territories east and west of the river, uniting the two into one. In their return to the opposite shore, the Transjordanians commemorate their bond to the western tribes—not only the bond of contiguous land or ethnicity, but a bond that is constituted by the presence of YHWH Himself. Like the stones of the earlier story, this altar conveys a message to future generations about YHWH's people. Furthermore, the textualization of Israel's dispute over this altar of "witness" enables not only the altar but also its story to become a witness to later generations of Israel, reminding them that Israel is bound together not only by geographical proximity, but by the presence of the one God, YHWH, in whom they all have a share.

Israel's Process of Obedience

In these two stories, Israel must continue to struggle to discover what form its faithfulness to YHWH will take as it confronts two further dilemmas of obedience. Through the aftermath of the Gibeonites' deceptive ploy and the questions raised by the Transjordanian altar, Israel continues to deal with the surprises and tensions involved in learning to live before YHWH in the land and within the Law. Even as it desires to act in obedience, Israel errs in making a treaty with the Gibeonites, but the text brings the reader alongside Israel to observe as it rightly judges the precedence of oath over *ḥerem*—and mercy over anger—when it discovers the truth. By depicting the tension-riddled yet open dialogue that follows the western tribes' initially explosive reaction to the eastern tribes' altar, the text offers a model for settling inner-Israelite disputes through discussion rather than by a hasty resort to violence.

The depiction of a process of deliberation leading to a positive outcome in these two stories suggests that even as Israel strives to maintain its faithfulness to YHWH, these depictions of Israel's own imperfect judgment should make Israel aware that swift action in response to sin must be balanced with careful investigation prior to the execution of punishment, if Israel is to avoid compounding transgression with transgression. Constructed around crises of obedience unmitigated by a word from on high, these two narratives direct Israel to the deep well of its knowledge of YHWH, of His Law, and of Israel's own history with Him as resources for its ongoing corporate life even when it lacks YHWH's immediate guidance.

FOUR

The Extent of Israel's Occupation of the Land

Thus far, I have examined the theme of Israel's obedience to YHWH in relation to relatively self-contained stories. In contrast, no single story neatly encapsulates the ambivalence exhibited by the book of Joshua in its portrayal of Israel's taking of the land. Especially in the latter section of the book, the text varies in its presentation of the extent to which Israel faithfully succeeds in claiming its inheritance in Canaan. Beginning in chapter 11 and continuing through the end of the book, a number of summaries and scattered statements join together to form a composite picture. The problem is, some of this material depicts a thorough and decisive taking of the land of Canaan, presenting the "conquest" as a thing of the past—a task completed within Joshua's lifetime. In contrast, other texts declare bluntly that the peoples of the land have yet to be fully expelled even after Joshua has reached old age. The contents of these various statements cannot honestly be reconciled, no matter how hard the reader may try. We can justifiably ask, then, what this clash of depictions means—why these portraits of partial conquest stand alongside statements of unmitigated victory. What are we to make of this mixed portrait of the taking of the land?

Robert Polzin offers one possible solution, setting up a stark contrast between the opening of chapter 13, with its portrait of unfinished conquest, and the sweeping statement of fulfillment that concludes the division of the land in chapter 21.[1] For Polzin, the two elements—complete fulfillment of the promises and total conquest versus an incomplete occupation of the land—stand in irreconcilable tension. In his view, these perspectives were intentionally juxtaposed in a way that makes the former seem impossibly ridiculous.[2] Instead of a completely successful conquest of the land, the latter section of the book of Joshua (chaps. 13–21) depicts a partial fulfillment of YHWH's promises, mirroring Israel's and Joshua's imperfect obedience to YHWH's commands in the first section of the book.[3] By the time the reader reaches the statement at the end of chapter 21, then, the sweeping portrait of fulfillment it offers has been rendered absurd by what precedes. According to Polzin, the statement of total fulfillment made in 21:43–45 "must be immediately and categorically denied by the reader if he chooses to continue to read and accept the basic ideological position of the text before him."[4] In short, "the Book of Joshua is scarcely intelligible if 21:41–43 is not read in an ironic sense."[5]

Polzin's adamance on this point pushes one to ask whether this is necessarily the case, however. Indeed, if the reader accepts Polzin's argument that the book of Joshua plays out a battle between the voice of critical traditionalism and the voice of authoritarian dogmatism, his conclusion may be inescapable. Yet one can easily argue in favor of other possible models for discussing the relationship between the "contradictory voices" in the book. If Israel genuinely is exploring and coming to occupy both Law and land, as Polzin aptly observes, why must the perspectives in the book exist in aggressive competition? The irreconcilable conflict seen by Polzin exists only at the level of the informational content of these varying statements about the extent of Israel's occupation of the land. Yet we need not take these statements as flatly factual disputes between two ideologies locked in a contest of assertion and counter-assertion. Instead, given that Polzin views the text itself as engaged in hermeneutical reflection on Israel's occupation of land and Law, it seems that a more apt model of communication for these coexisting voices would be one of exploratory dialogical difference. If, in the book of Joshua, Israel is making a foray into the unfamiliar territory of both land and Torah, these differing voices contribute varying perspectives on how to map out the complex terrain of Israel's life in the land, led and sustained by the Law, in relationship with YHWH.

As I have argued in the second chapter of this work, the point at which contrasting depictions grate against each other in the text should be precisely the starting point for seeking the meaning of the juxtaposition. It is not sufficient merely to trace the separate origins of these differing accounts by explaining how they came into existence, or to figure out how to make them say the same thing, or to relinquish them as hopelessly conflicting. These solutions, while possible avenues of exploration, remain inadequate as explanations of the complex and carefully crafted text of Joshua, in my opinion. Their insufficiency does not bring us to a dead end, however; rather, it directs us to turn our efforts toward exploring the *meaning* of the differing statements and juxtaposed content, which is the goal of this chapter. Instead of attempting to eliminate the conflict regarding the extent of Israel's taking of the land in the book of Joshua or giving it up as a lost cause, this chapter explores what these varying accounts contribute *together* to Israel's telling of its earliest days in the land.

I will argue that the redactor of the book of Joshua uses the statements that emphasize the complete, successful taking of the land to communicate YHWH's complete faithfulness to Israel in the fulfillment of His promise of the land. The point of these statements is that YHWH did not fail Israel; He gave what He promised. On the other hand, the statements that indicate that parts of the land in fact were not taken, or that parts of the land still remain to be taken, are used by the redactor to convey a dual message. At times, they emphasize the *contingency* of the occupation of the land in relation to Israel, and the need for Israel's action in response to YHWH[6]—although significantly, they do not yet fault Israel with disobedience for failing to complete the task of settlement. Complementing this, though, is their assurance to the reader of YHWH's control of the situation, and of His continuing work on Israel's behalf to give Israel full possession of the land even beyond Joshua's lifetime. The emphasis here falls on the *ongoing* rather than *occasional* nature of YHWH's advocacy of and exercise of power on behalf of Israel.

The redactor's incorporation of these two groups of material creates a striking tension in the story overall, both in the depiction of YHWH's action and character, and of Israel's responsibilities. On the one hand, YHWH both *has already done* what He has promised, and *will continue to do* as He has promised. On the other hand, Israel too must act to receive or participate fully in this prior work of YHWH's. This literary strategy effectively places Israel's fate always in the balance—always hanging upon Joshua's proffered choice between serving YHWH and serving other gods (24:14–15). It both leaves room for continued obedience on Israel's part, parallel to YHWH's ongoing exercise of faithfulness to His elect, and—as implied in the notes about the subjection of the remaining Canaanites in Joshua 15–17—opens up the more ominous possibility that Israel can yet cease to participate in YHWH's work,[7] and that a persistent failure to act will become disobedience on Israel's part.[8]

Such an understanding of these juxtaposed themes has implications for our reading of the book which mesh with our previous insights regarding Israel's mixed obedience and disobedience throughout the book of Joshua. Here, as elsewhere, YHWH leaves room for Israel's shortcomings in the midst of His own perfect plans and standards for His people. This "room" is reflected in the choice laid before Israel in chapter 23, with regard to the taking of the rest of the land, and on the grander scale of their overall allegiance to YHWH in chapter 24. Acceptance of YHWH's gifts and of YHWH's lordship cannot be separated.[9] Similarly, both YHWH's gift of the land and YHWH's rule over Israel cannot be separated from Israel's identity. YHWH has called Israel to live up to and live into its calling in new ways in the land, separating itself from the peoples of the land and the alternative allegiances they represent. He has called Israel to be a holy people, obedient to and belonging to Him alone. When Israel chooses not to live into this calling, it also fails to experience all the benefits extended to it as YHWH's people. We see this already taking place within the book of Joshua, and even more so in the book of Judges, descending finally, at the end of DtrH, to Israel's separation from the land given by YHWH because of Israel's failure to live out the implications of its identity as YHWH's elect. Israel's straying to other gods is not a matter of indifference, a choice of another possible identity, but rather its undoing—Israel's loss of its only true identity.[10] YHWH's choice and YHWH's gifts are prior to anything Israel chooses to be or fails to be.[11] YHWH has already fully given all that He has promised, the book makes clear. Israel can now accept the gift of the land and continue to live into it, to "occupy" it—a task that, with equal transparency, the book of Joshua depicts as an ongoing process rather than as the result of a single military campaign—or Israel can fail to live into this gift and thus, ultimately, fail to receive the fullness of what YHWH has already granted as Israel's portion. The paradoxical portrait of Israel's settlement of Canaan thus created deserves to be explored and articulated in all of its complexity.

Framing the Study: The Clash between Joshua 11–12 and Joshua 13

How the Texts Clash and Why: The Redactor's Theological Message

The clash between Joshua 11–12 and Joshua 13 exemplifies the larger-scale conflict throughout the latter part of the book within this theme of the extent of Israel's taking of the land. The common division of the book of Joshua into two parts, between chapters 1–12 and chapters 13–24, can distract the reader from this juxtaposition—perhaps the most jarring collision of these contrasting themes in the entire book. Here, the sweeping, victorious summaries of chapters 11 and 12 run up against YHWH's declaration at the start of chapter 13 that much land remains to be taken.[12] This clash is not played out with excessive subtlety, as if the redactor has, in a somewhat embarrassed manner, spliced together two disparate accounts. Rather, the placement of these texts practically parades the collision before the reader's eyes, bringing these two perspectives together precisely at the point of maximum dissonance.

This sharp juxtaposition suggests the work of a careful, intentional redactor, mindful of the content and context of the texts that he is bringing together. Like the narratives of obedience and failure to obey that we described in the previous two chapters, the clash seems too obvious and effective to result accidentally from the clumsy work of a careless compiler. In fact, it would hardly be possible to choose a pair from the book that would convey the tension between these two "perspectives" on the extent of Israel's occupation of the land more clearly. Instead, the text exhibits here a meaningful juxtaposition of source materials, set into place by a redactor who conveys a particular theological message by his literary actions. The portrait that he has created to convey his message is a portrait of "Israel in the balance," enjoying partial receipt of YHWH's promises, yet continually poised to live into their fullness. The text that he forms from his sources tells more than a story about a shared past; it serves as a "state of the union address" perpetually expounded, always addressing Israel as the people who live in-between: between promise and fulfillment, mercy and judgment, now and not yet. Israel is always defined at its very roots as the people constituted by YHWH's choosing and dependent/reliant upon YHWH's promises. Yet Israel can resist its YHWH-given identity and gifting, reluctant to stand out among the nations and do the hard work of receiving Torah and promises alike. It is from this position that the redactor compiles his text, the situation of exile and the uncertainty it brings.[13] He lives—as will an increasing number of YHWH's people—in separation from the land promised to the ancestors, "singing the songs of Zion" without any certainty that during his lifetime he will set foot in Jerusalem again. Yet this redactor writes in hope of Israel's restoration, recognizing that he can have such a hope only in dependence upon YHWH's promises and the ever-renewed opportunity for restoration that YHWH offers to Israel through them. He depicts an Israel that fails—and lives to tell about it, only because it sincerely repents and serves YHWH. By this image, this study painted in the medium of Israel's own stories of the past, he holds out a choice: the choice of obedience and the chance to experience again YHWH's favor. His theological solution to the situation of exile is at once timely and timeless: addressing the specific dilemma of his own generation in a way that enables the text to address future generations of Israel as well.

Details of the Text's Construction

The redactor's construction opens with the success of the Israelite campaigns against Canaan in Joshua 11:16–23—a rousing climax to the battles depicted in the former part of the book, which also makes a clear connection between this success and Joshua's obedience to Moses' commands. Although the boundaries and extent of the land claimed by Israel in the course of its military endeavors remain somewhat unclear, the summary at the end of chapter 11 implies a broad territorial and temporal scope to Israel's conquests, declaring their conclusion with a sense of comprehensive finality. The inclusion of the Gibeonites as the sole exception to Israel's no-mercy *ḥerem* policy (11:19), the mention of the lengthy process involved in taking the land (11:18), and finally, the interpretation of the bellicosity of the Canaanites as a sign of the Lord's purpose to destroy them (11:20) suggest that the referent of "all that land" in 11:16 is the full scope of territories taken by Joshua and the Israelites in battle. YHWH's promises are fulfilled; the land is taken; end of story.

A lengthy list of conquered kings follows, constituting the whole of chapter 12 and further detailing Israel's success—only to collide a moment later with YHWH's startling statement at the start of chapter 13 that Joshua is old and that much land still remains to be taken (13:1, along with vv. 2–7)! The text's confident summation of Joshua's finished work and complete obedience regarding the taking of the land (11:23) stands uneasily alongside the text's report of YHWH's own "decommissioning" of Joshua and description of the work that remains to be done (13:1–7). Framed as a retrospective on the conquest spoken in YHWH's own voice, this summary is addressed directly to

Joshua. After noting Joshua's advanced age—evoking the long process of conquest—and briefly tallying Israel's victories, YHWH discusses the problem of the quantity of land that "still remains"—the territories not yet conquered by the Israelites (13:1). The Lord's declaration that "very much of the land still remains to be possessed" clashes harshly with the multitudinous *all*'s and the lengthy king list of the preceding two chapters. While the conquest *under Joshua* may be over, YHWH seems to say, Israel's taking possession of the land YHWH has given it is a process that must continue beyond Joshua's death. At this point, the text expresses no concern about this incomplete work, nor does it frame it as a threat either to Israel's safety or its fidelity to YHWH. It is simply as if the taking of the land shifts suddenly from being an open-and-shut case to remaining an open-ended project that will continue to require YHWH's—and Israel's—attention.

YHWH's Speech in Joshua 13:1–7

The speech itself begins with YHWH's dual highlighting of Joshua's advancing years and the quantity of land remaining to be possessed by Israel (11:1), but how this pairing should influence our understanding of the tone and purpose of the speech is not immediately clear. The emphasis on Joshua's old age combined with the incompleteness of his commissioned task of taking the land could, on the one hand, be understood as a reprimand, charging Joshua with laxity or slowness in fulfilling his appointed task. Understood in this way, YHWH would be charging Joshua with failing to finish successfully the work he was given. On the other hand, this pairing might function primarily to offer a portrait of the taking of the land which explicitly contrasts with the one that concludes chapter 11. In this case, the speech offers an alternative to the narrative that Israel completely took possession of the land under the leadership of Joshua, presenting it instead as a process begun under Joshua's leadership but extending beyond his lifetime.

Hawk offers a straightforwardly negative take on the contrast, framed in his language of "competing plots"; he notes the movement from fulfillment and success in chapter 11 to nonfulfillment and fragmentation in chapter 13.¹⁴ For him, assertions of completeness here and elsewhere in the book of Joshua cannot be taken at face value, as they are undermined by counter-assertions of incompleteness.¹⁵ Rather than offering a complementary or mutually coherent message, the latter cancels out the former. Hawk's only observations regarding the address of YHWH's critical speech to Joshua in particular, rather than Israel at large, have to do with a negative comparison he perceives between the leadership of Joshua and that of Moses.¹⁶

Mitchell seems unsure of how to read the tone of YHWH's speech in chapter 13, labeling the text as a "rebuke," because of the unfinished work it highlights, yet also describes the tone of the passage as "very matter-of-fact," suggesting a lack of censure in YHWH's words.¹⁷ In the midst of this uncertainty, he does, laudably, recognize the insufficiency of explaining the differing land conquests by origin or redaction alone, and the need to read the contrasting statements of complete and incomplete conquest in concert with other tensions that run through the book.¹⁸

In contrast, Butler offers an unequivocally positive evaluation of Joshua's standing before YHWH in this speech, since "even though much remains to be done (13:1–6), the victory can be described as total because the work of Joshua has been carried out in total faithfulness."¹⁹ For him, Joshua appears here as a paragon of obedience.²⁰ This still leaves him, though, with the challenge of relating the contrasting portraits of the extent of the taking of the land in chapters 11 and 13,²¹ and explaining why YHWH seems to be relieving Joshua of his duties here in the face of the incomplete work that Joshua 13:1–7 describes.

Despite the initial inclination to blame Joshua for the lack of total conquest since it is he whom YHWH addresses, the text in fact suggests no shaming or reprimand of either Joshua or Israel at this point for the fact that "a great deal of land remains to be possessed" (13:1). Further exploration of the contents of the speech beyond its introductory statements helps to illuminate its purpose. The bulk of the speech, found in 13:2–6, lists portions of land yet to be taken by the Israelites, along with the names of the people-groups that inhabit this land. Following these lists are YHWH's assurances to Israel that *He Himself* will continue to work on their behalf in securing the land (v. 6b), and the consequent command that Joshua should now move on to allocating this land to the Israelites in advance of YHWH's action: "I myself will dispossess them from before the children of Israel; in view of this [*raq*], allot it to Israel as an inheritance, just as I have commanded you" (6b). Finally, the passage concludes with a divine command to begin the process of the allotment of the land, specifically to the nine and a half tribes (v. 7). The adverb *ʿattâ* redirects the reader's attention to the task at hand for Joshua and indicates that this verse does not merely continue the thought of the former—that is, the commanded allotment of the land specified in verses 2–6. Rather, YHWH's command in verse 7 initiates the *overall* process of dividing the conquered territories and identifies Joshua's present task in distinction from his former military commission. The narrative then pauses for a flashback to Moses' prior division of the Cisjordanian territories among the other tribes (vv. 8–33), providing an antecedent for Joshua's action, which commences in chapter 14.[22]

In light of this broader context, we can better understand the purpose of the initial divine statement of Joshua's age and the incompleteness of Israel's possession of the land. As we have seen, the passage does not dwell on the consequences of the initial statement for either the reader's or YHWH's evaluation of Joshua. Instead, it shifts very quickly to the subject of the unclaimed or unconquered territories. Furthermore, Joshua is not disciplined in any way for the fact that the Israelites have yet to take possession of certain portions of the land. Rather, as verse 6b shows, the point of the passage is not Joshua's failure but YHWH's ongoing faithfulness; not Joshua's inaction but YHWH's persistently continuing action. YHWH acknowledges the land yet to be taken, in order to assure Israel that He will continue to enact His promise that Israel will possess the land.[23]

Seen in this context, YHWH's remark upon Joshua's age serves not as a reprimand, but to *shift Joshua's role* from that of leader in battle to that of victor and conqueror, who distributes what has been claimed by warfare. This lack of censure is reflected further in the fact that YHWH does not command Joshua to continue or complete the taking of the land, as if Joshua himself is able to make up what is lacking in what he has led Israel to accomplish thus far. YHWH is, in effect, granting Joshua an honorable discharge upon successful completion of his military role. The transition from era of conquest to division of the land, and the rest that it brings with it, also marks a transition in Joshua's role.[24] He is now to lead Israel into its rest—a state that repeatedly appears in the text as characterizing the postwar settlement period (11:23, 21:44, 22:4, 23:1)—while YHWH reasserts His role as warrior on Israel's behalf.[25] In response to this promised action, YHWH requires Israel's confidence in His future action through its proleptic division of the land not yet taken. It is YHWH Himself, not Joshua, who will complete the task of dispossessing the Canaanites.

The Purpose of the Contrast

This passage, with its unselfconscious statement of incompleteness and its emphasis on YHWH's ongoing—and therefore unfinished—action, stands at odds with the text's insistence only two chapters earlier that Joshua took the entire land and rest ensued. Several significant differences found through comparison of the two passages point toward how this contrast functions within the book of Joshua. First, the earlier passage gives a more central role to Joshua's agency in the taking of the land. There, Joshua is the subject of the two main verbs of the sentence: *wayyiqqaḥ yĕhôšuaʿ ʾet-kol hāʾāreṣ . . . wayyittĕnâ yĕhôšuaʿ lĕnaḥălâ lĕyiśrāʾēl*; he *took* the entire land and he *gave* it to Israel (11:23). The emphasis falls upon Joshua's victorious actions. In the passage in chapter 13, on the other hand, Joshua is, first of all, *old*, not active; the only thing he is "doing" is advancing in years (*bāʾ bayyāmîm*, 13:1)! When he does receive a task in the course of the speech, it is a task that is not in itself complete or self-contained, but rather serves as preparation for YHWH's eventual action. That is, Joshua divides the land among the tribes in anticipation of YHWH's driving out of the peoples who inhabit it (13:6–7). It is YHWH who will ultimately complete the task of taking the land, not Joshua.

Second, the passage in chapter 11 presents YHWH's speech as a past promise transmitted faithfully in written form by Moses and faithfully enacted by YHWH through Joshua (11:23). YHWH's written word is effective through human agents. In 13:1–7, however, YHWH directly speaks anew to Joshua, and takes personal responsibility for completing the action of dispossessing the Canaanites. This word comes to Joshua as *present* divine speech instead of through the written word he carries with him, giving the sense that YHWH's plan for Israel is still unfolding rather than squared away neatly at Joshua's passing. To put it another way, YHWH's speech in chapter 13 is not an unalterable map of Israel's destiny set down for all time, but instead demonstrates how YHWH will actively and personally intervene in shaping Israel's future.

Finally, and perhaps most obviously, the first passage envisions the taking of the land as a task completed down to the letter under Joshua himself, while the second passage presents it as a process that must extend beyond Joshua's lifetime. The first gives the reader a sense of finality with the successful taking of "all the land," while the second unsettles the reader with the notice that "much remains to be taken." Even as the first conveys the power of the divine word and the victorious completion of a task by a man whose way the Lord has caused to prosper, the latter conveys the frailty of human life and its brevity paired with the impression of a divine plan that surpasses and cannot be contained within such finitude. This divine plan, though, also acknowledges and works with mortal creatures, making up what is lacking in both human ability (the final eradication of the Canaanites), and in human longevity (YHWH's work on behalf of Israel will continue long after Joshua has been gathered to his ancestors).

What might have given rise to these two different perspectives, these two different portraits of the extent to which Joshua brought Israel into possession of the land of Canaan? I would argue that the passage at the end of chapter 11 is marked particularly by its concern for complete fulfillment of YHWH's past words to Israel and the sufficiency of that divine speech, as faithfully transmitted by Moses and obeyed by Joshua. As a result, it casts a vision of an ideal situation, a one-to-one match between word and fulfillment within Joshua's lifetime. The passage at the start of chapter 13, on the other hand, is not so much a more "realistic" portrait as it is one that offers a different perspective on the divine word. Here, the divine word comes anew in a transaction that interposes YHWH's action at the point at which Joshua is no longer able to continue acting as warrior, accommodating itself to human finitude and frailty.[26] In the first passage, all the perfection and success that might be expected of the faithful leader aided by YHWH shines through. In contrast, the second reflects the situation of God's people as we have seen it so often throughout the book, in which YHWH's intervention is needed to make up for the points at which human shortcomings and weaknesses would otherwise spell Israel's doom. Thus, these two passages are telling us two different things about YHWH through their contrasting portraits: namely, that YHWH's word is perfect and does not fail, but that YHWH accommodates fallible human beings. At the same time, they share in the proclamation of YHWH's faithfulness to Israel, exhibited in diverse ways.

The shift from completeness to incompleteness between chapters 11–12 and 13 in the book of Joshua does not serve as a condemnation of Joshua or Israel. Instead, it provides an opportunity for YHWH's assurance of His continued faithfulness to and advocacy of Israel: "I will myself drive them out from before the Israelites" (13:6). In relation to chapters 11 and 12, chapter 13 changes the focus, shifting the emphasis from Joshua's obedient performance of his task to YHWH's ongoing action on Israel's behalf, extending beyond Joshua's brief lifetime. Joshua's role, now, is only obediently to "allot the land to Israel for an inheritance, as I have commanded you" (v. 7). Joshua is not shamed by his discharge at the start of chapter 13 but rather relativized. YHWH's speech shifts the focus from demonstrating the efficacy of YHWH's word and lauding the obedient actions of Joshua, so recently affirmed in chapter 11 (and implicitly in chapter 12), to indicating Israel's ongoing need for *YHWH's* presence and action. The text honors the obedience and accomplishments of Israel's human leaders, yet relieves them of the burden of ultimate importance by refocusing attention on

YHWH's overarching action on Israel's behalf, which both includes and exceeds human activity.

Intimations of Incompleteness

This initial comparison between the triumphant conclusion of chapter 11 and the uncertain new beginning of chapter 13 functions as a microcosm of the tensions present in the land theme overall throughout the book. Generally, though, these statements of completeness and incompleteness do not stand on such equal footing in terms of their position in the text. While statements emphasizing completeness fairly uniformly tend to be situated as conclusions or summaries at pivotal points in the text (e.g., 11:23, 21:43–45), those that note the presence of Canaanite remnants among the Israelites are strewn throughout chapters 15–17 rather unevenly, with further intimations of an incomplete expulsion of the Canaanites in chapter 23, and an exhortation to action directed at several tribes that have not yet occupied their territory in chapter 18—the only indication of incomplete occupation that is not directly linked with an ongoing Canaanite presence.[27] Because these statements lack a consistent arrangement and format, they must be "collected" and evaluated individually, taking into account both their form and context, before their contribution as a group to the land theme in the book can be properly understood.

This group of statements about surviving Canaanites can be subdivided further into two groups: one of which names specific locations where Canaanites continue to live within specific tribal territories,[28] and the other of which indicates a general need for the continued expulsion of Canaanites from the land.[29] We will begin by examining this first subgroup of more specific statements, and then turn to consider the second, more general set.

Canaanite Pockets within Israel's Territory

While the precise phrasing of the statements about "pockets" of Canaanites remaining within Israel's tribal territories varies, most of these imply lack of success on Israel's part in evicting them.[30] Only in 16:10, where the Israelites are said to have successfully subjected the Canaanites to corvée labor, is it unclear whether their failure to evict the Canaanites is a matter of inability or choice. In the majority of cases of Canaanite holdouts, however, Israel is *unable* rather than unwilling to evict them (15:63, 17:12–13), even meeting with active—and apparently successful—resistance (17:12–13).

This Canaanite "determination" or "resolve" to remain in the land is a factor that has no parallel in the book prior to this point. Quite the contrary, Joshua has YHWH's promise from the outset that "no one will be able to stand against you all the days of your life" (Josh 1:5). The only successful resistance Israel has thus far encountered resulted from YHWH's wrath following Achan's sin (Josh 7:1–5). Nowhere have the Canaanites been credited with the sort of intentional and effective resistance encountered here.

Following the note about Canaanite resolve to remain in the land in 17:12–13, a dialogue proceeds in which the Joseph tribes complain to Joshua of their cramped quarters (17:14–18). The ensuing dialogue between Joshua and the relevant tribes is unparalleled elsewhere among the Canaanite notices in the book, and seems to be appended as an explanation and exposition of the unique Canaanite "willfulness" encountered by the Manassites—probably spliced in from a different source, as the abrupt change of subject from "the Manassites" and their territory in 17:1–13 to the "Joseph tribes" in verses 14–18 suggests.[31]

According to Joshua's argument, the descendents of Joseph *do* have the ability to drive out these Canaanites, just like any others; it is, in fact, their certainty that they are *unable* to drive out these Canaanites that stands in the way. Joshua seizes upon the positive angle to their grumblings, which initially spurred their complaint: "We are a numerous people, and the Lord has blessed us abundantly" (17:14). He affirms their strength in numbers and implicitly their blessing by the Lord. But he does not accept their argument that their portion is too small for them; instead, he cuts to the heart of the problem. The Joseph tribes have not occupied all of the territory allotted to them, for fear of the well-equipped Canaanites who dwell in it, as their hesitant response reveals (17:16). Joshua turns their argument on its head, seizing upon their numerical strength as the grounds for their ability to clear the land in 17:17–18. If the Joseph tribes genuinely believe that it is the Lord who has blessed them with such numbers that their current territory bursts at the seams, then they should act upon their trust in YHWH's blessing and take hold of the inheritance that is theirs. Joshua even assures them of their success: "Though the Canaanites have chariots of iron and are strong, you can drive them out" (v. 18). The scene ends on this open, hortatory note.

Within its broader literary context, we can take Joshua's confidence in Israel's ability to drive out the Canaanites and occupy the land as resting on the divine speech of chapter 13, in which the Lord asserts that He Himself will take charge of driving out the remaining peoples of the land on Israel's behalf. Joshua's answer reminds the Joseph tribes that the Lord's blessings are not something that can be claimed without accepting the responsibility they entail. The Lord has already allotted to each tribe its portion, but each must trustingly and actively receive that gift to benefit from it. This narrative suggests that in spite of the Canaanite strength expressed in 17:12–13 and verses 14–18, even the best-armed Canaanites would be no match for Israel if it were to act in faithfulness to YHWH's promises.

Because it integrates a segment of dialogue, the example in chapter 17 is the most expansive of the notes about remaining pockets of Canaanites; the two notices in chapters 15 and 16 are much briefer. Joshua 15:63 seems targeted at explaining the ongoing presence of Jebusites in Jerusalem among the Judahites,[32] even "to this day."[33] Rather than attributing the existence of this Canaanite remnant to fear or reluctance on the part of the Judahites, the text simply tells us that the Judahites "were not able" to dislodge the Canaanites from this city. Similarly, Joshua 16:10 offers no causation for the remnant of Canaanites in Gezer, though here the Ephraimites "did not" dislodge them rather than "were unable" as in 15:63. As in 17:13, the Canaanites that remain are subjected to corvée labor—a situation that occurs in two out of the three remnant notes in the book of Joshua, but which appears more frequently in the passage listing Canaanite remnants in Judges 1 (vv. 28,

THE EXTENT OF ISRAEL'S OCCUPATION OF THE LAND

30, 33, 35). These scattered notes in Joshua may indicate the open possibility that the Israelites will still act in full obedience to YHWH and continue to drive out the majority of the Canaanites.[34] In contrast, the consolidated block in Judges, especially with its greater proportion of subject Canaanites, concedes a less desirable state of affairs, pointing ahead to Israel's reprimand at Bochim in Judges 2.[35]

Joshua 18:1–10

Israel's failure to complete the task of occupying the land is most openly criticized in 18:1–10, where Joshua admonishes the remaining seven tribes who have not yet received their allotments with the words "How long will you neglect to go in and take possession of the land that the Lord, the God of your ancestors, has given you?" (18:3). Strikingly, this is also the single occasion in the latter portion of the book in which Israel, having fallen short, immediately rises to the challenge and acts in obedience, consistent with its record of repentance in the narratives of the first part of the book. In contrast to the exemplary actions of Caleb (14:6–15), Caleb's daughter (15:13–19), and Zelophahad's daughters (16:6–9), who have come forward of their own initiative to claim their portions, these seven tribes have not yet acted to occupy the land that has been given by the Lord (18:2).[36] Joshua leads them into obedient action by initiating the process of settlement, directing representatives from each tribe to form a surveying party and map out the remaining land (18:4–6). Once this task has been completed, Joshua casts lots for the remaining territory, dividing it among the seven tribes (18:8–10). Thus, this narrative turns out to be self-contained, in that the rebuke initially offered by Joshua is met with obedient action such that the situation of neglect is remedied.[37]

Overlapping Fragments

What we are left with after examining these collected fragments from chapters 13–18 (see table 4.1) is a handful of puzzle pieces that do not fit together to form a uniform picture. Instead, the description of the Canaanite presence in the land consists of brief, scattered accounts, such that no single party is clearly made responsible for the fact that pockets of Canaanites remain in the midst of the Israelite allotments. YHWH acknowledges the ongoing presence of Canaanites but absolves Joshua from responsibility for continuing the conquest, taking the task upon Himself instead in chapter 13, prior to the division of the land. The Canaanites exercise initiative of their own in continuing to occupy certain cities within Israel's territory; they essentially refuse to be ousted (17:12–13). Could the tribes overcome the Canaanites' resistance to their eviction? In the case of the Joseph tribes, which we have been considering above, the text offers a mixed response. These tribes, the text indicates in 17:12–13, do not succeed in driving out the Canaanites from certain cities within their territory. Yet in the same chapter, Joshua's discussion with the Joseph tribes asserts that the Joseph tribes *are* strong enough that "you *will* dispossess them, even though they have iron chariots" (17:18). The apparent implication is that if the Joseph tribes should overcome their fear and take on the heavily armed Canaanites, YHWH will indeed lead them to victory and into possession of their land when they act upon His promise of presence.

The text offers the reader the pieces needed to conclude that YHWH is still ready and willing to act on Israel's behalf in warfare but will oppose the Canaanites not by supernatural means, as in the case of Jericho, but by the military action of the tribes themselves. When Israel refuses to confront the Canaanites, it misses out on the benefits of YHWH's advocacy, as the scenario involving the Joseph tribes at the end of chapter 17 suggests.[38] Notably, however, the book of Joshua does not lay the blame for the Canaanite remnants on any single party, nor does it suggest that their presence is a necessary or permanent state of affairs. Rather, it supplies the reader with an assemblage of brief snapshots and fragmentary information—none of which presents a complete picture in itself—that relates to the outcome of Israel's settlement of the land, and hints at other possible outcomes.

In relation to the occupation of the land, the book of Joshua presents a subtle dance of divine action and human reaction. Even though YHWH is the only one who is fully capable of giving what He has

Table 4.1. Summary of Intimations of Incompleteness

Reference	Dramatis Personae	Form of Statement	Corvée Labor?	Summary
13:1–7	YHWH, Joshua	"Much land remains to be taken," "I myself will drive out the inhabitants of XYZ"	No	Canaanites remain, but YHWH Himself will drive them out
15:63	Judahites, Jebusites	"not able"	No	Judahites unable to remove Jebusites
16:10	People of Ephraim, Canaanites of Gezer	"Did not dislodge"	Yes	Ephraimites
17:11–13	Manassites; Canaanites of Beth Shan, Ibleam, Dor, En-Dor, Taanach, Megiddo	Canaanites "decided to remain"; Manassites "could not occupy"	Yes	Manassites unable to evict Canaanites who decide to stay
17:14–18	People of Joseph, Perizzites & Rephaites, Canaanites of the plain around Beth Shean & Jezreel	Dialogue between Joshua and the people of Joseph, in which Joshua asserts their ability to occupy their allotted land	No	People of Joseph hesitate to occupy their land due to Canaanites with "iron chariots"; Joshua urges them to claim their land

promised, Israel has more than a merely inert role as the recipient of His promises. Israel cannot stand passive on the banks of the Jordan while the "hornet" accomplishes its work and the Canaanites are thrown into turmoil, then simply stroll in and start pitching its tents. The disobedience of the wilderness generation in their refusal to enter the land shows that Israel has the option of rejecting YHWH's benefits. One thing that should be made clear, though, is that Israel does not have the power to reject YHWH's choosing altogether. Whether or not Israel wants to live into its identity at any particular moment, Israel *is* chosen by YHWH. Israel is not free to break its bond with YHWH and enter into relationships with other gods if it tires of YHWH's election. Israel does not have the choice of becoming like any other nation. Only within the boundaries of chosenness can Israel choose.[39] Every action and decision that Israel makes takes place within the perimeter of the covenant and its consequences of blessing and curse. Israel can choose prosperity or damnation as its lot, but it cannot escape YHWH's persistent gaze, its position as the apple of YHWH's eye. Such divine attentiveness can be both blessing and curse, depending on the response of the recipients.

So Israel must respond, since even inaction is a choice—a choice to hold back from receiving YHWH's promises, which require Israel's action as answer to YHWH's initiative. Israel must cross the Jordan, confront the Canaanites, destroy cities as commanded, divide the land, clear the hill country. Yet YHWH is present in or alongside Israel's action all along the way: at the parting of Jordan and the crossing on dry land, at the fall of the walls of Jericho, as the chooser of the lots, as the ultimate agent in driving out the Canaanites. Israel never acts alone, but Israel *must* act if it is to receive the benefits of the covenant rather than the curses. And as Israel acts, YHWH gives—gives a miraculous parting of the river, gives the stunning removal of the walls of Jericho, gives victory against better-armed kings and opponents, gives the land.

It is in Israel's receiving of the land that this drama reaches its climax among the themes of the book. In the receiving of the land is tied up Israel's obedience or disobedience, Israel's acknowledgment of its identity as YHWH's people or its apostasy with other gods. If Israel takes the land that YHWH has given it and drives out its inhabitants, Israel will enjoy all the peace and prosperity showered upon it by YHWH. If, on the other hand, Israel abandons its struggle against the remaining Canaanites and fails to occupy the land it has been given, Israel will stray after the gods of other peoples and risk the wrath of its own covenant partner. In the tradition of incomplete occupation woven into the land theme, we find the open possibility that Israel will fail to fulfill its part of the bargain. The text leaves us with a tension between YHWH's promise to drive out the rest of the inhabitants of the land, and the notices that tell us that some remain "to this day." This is where

THE EXTENT OF ISRAEL'S OCCUPATION OF THE LAND

not only the land theme but the book of Joshua as a whole leaves Israel: affirming its choice of YHWH under the leadership of Joshua but warned that it *cannot* choose YHWH. At some point, Israel will lapse in its faithfulness to YHWH despite its declared choice, and when it does, Israel must suffer the wrath of its "possessive God" (24:19–20) before it can experience YHWH's mercy and redemption again.

A Finished Project

In the face of these intimations of incompleteness and the threat of Israel's fallibility, the latter section of the book also contains passages that emphasize the completeness of YHWH's giving of the land and the subjection of Israel's opponents. These statements, which are found in 21:43–45; 23:1, 3–4; and 24:11–13, vary in form and content just as those indicating incompleteness did. The summary in 21:43–45 is the most programmatic of these, repeatedly emphasizing the completeness of YHWH's fulfillment of His promises; in contrast, the passage in chapter 24 simply speaks of the dispossession of the Canaanite nations as a past work of YHWH, placing no particular emphasis on the fact. A somewhat more complicated picture emerges from chapter 23, in which some verses suggest that "YHWH has granted rest to Israel" (*hēnîaḥ YHWH lĕyiśrāʾēl*, 23:1)[40] and has conquered the nations (23:4), while other verses indicate that some Canaanites remain to be dealt with by YHWH and Israel (23:5, 12–13). As with the indications of incompleteness, these passages must be considered individually before their corporate place within the book can be assessed.

Joshua 21:43–45

The statement in 21:43–45 serves as the counterpart to the summarizing statement at the end of Joshua 11 for the latter portion of the book, but encompasses a vaster scope.[41] While 11:23 recapped Joshua's successful completion of his task, this statement has a more comprehensive summation in view, emphasizing the completeness of *all* of

YHWH's work in relation to the land: "43. So the Lord gave to Israel *all* the land that He had sworn to give their ancestors, and they took possession of it and occupied it. 44. The Lord gave rest to them all around, according to *all* that He swore to their ancestors, and no one stood against them from among *all* of their enemies; *all* of their enemies, the Lord gave into their hand. 45. Not a thing went unfulfilled from the entire good word that the Lord had spoken to the house of Israel; *everything* [he said] happened." To convey the strongest possible emphasis on completeness, the text uses the word *kol* at every opportunity—five times in the space of three verses. Further reinforcement comes from two statements of negation (*wĕlōʾ-ʿāmad ʾîš*, "no one stood," in v. 44; and *lōʾ-nāpal dābār*, "not a thing went unfulfilled," in v. 45), which fill up any gaps that might be left amongst the "alls." The emphatic tone of this passage serves it well in the pivotal position that it occupies in the text. The location of this statement between the division of the land and the parting of ways between the Transjordanian and Cisjordanian tribes sets it as a significant divider between the era of conquest, encompassing the period of warfare and the subsequent distribution of the conquered territories under Joshua, and the era of settlement, marked by the dispersion of the tribes to their territories and the end of Joshua's leadership of united Israel. While 11:23 served as a hinge, looking back to the taking of the land in the preceding chapters and looking ahead to the division of the land in the following chapters, the statement in 21:43–45 marks the end of an era on a larger scale. Joshua's role after this point involves "tying up loose ends" and giving his parting speeches, no longer active seizure or settlement of the land. The conquest is over, and only Joshua's imminent death separates Israel from the era of the judges.

In some ways, this passage resembles the summary statement in 11:23 in that it projects a full realization of every one of YHWH's "good promises" to Israel with regard to the land.[42] Nonetheless, it differs significantly in its lack of mention of Joshua; instead, it focuses on divine agency, such that the primary action of the conquest is not the "taking" of the land by Joshua or Israel, but YHWH's "giving" of it (*wayyittēn YHWH*, 21:43). The statement in chapter 11 attaches the threefold chain of command—YHWH → Moses → Joshua—to the taking of the land, highlighting Joshua's obedient action in relation to the book of the Law. No mention is made of the book of the Law in 11:23, but the threefold chain of command noted above implies its presence, such that YHWH's word becomes the vehicle of His agency; it thereby puts Joshua's intermediary role in the forefront as agent of the Lord's past speech conveyed through Moses. In so doing, it hints at the latent presence of the book of the Law that bears Moses' words and that is to accompany and guide Joshua on his journey through the land, according to Joshua 1. In 21:43-45, on the other hand, the emphasis falls so strongly on YHWH's personal action that the text does not even mention Joshua's name.[43] YHWH serves as the subject for a total of five different verbs: giving land, rest, and power over enemies (vv. 43, 44); making an oath to the ancestors (vv. 43, 44); and speaking his intentions for Israel (v. 45). He features as the central actor in the passage.

YHWH is not the sole actor in this passage, however; Israel makes an appearance in 21:43-45 that has no parallel in 11:23. While the latter mentioned Israel only as a beneficiary of Joshua's actions with regard to the land, the former statement speaks of Israel as active in subduing and occupying the land (21:44) as the result of YHWH's gift of it. Rather than emphasizing the mediation of Joshua, then, this passage deals with YHWH's actions as directly benefiting Israel; not Joshua's faithfulness to YHWH, but rather YHWH's faithful fulfillment for Israel of the promises made to the ancestors (21:43) is in view here.

This summary statement strives to offer a seamless vision of YHWH's actions on Israel's behalf, with the effect of making it immensely clear that any shortcoming could not be a failure on YHWH's part. YHWH's faithful fulfillment of His promises is emphatically asserted, with every dimension of success explicitly stated lest any possible accusation of failure remain unanswered. The statement is so emphatic that it tempts some readers to wonder what, exactly, it is trying to hide; Polzin in particular finds it impossible to accept as anything other than sheer irony.[44] For him, Joshua 13-21 itself constitutes a critique of the statement in 21:43-45, and the ideology that grounds the former cannot be reconciled with that which grounds the latter.[45]

Does the tone and shape of the material within the book actually support this reading? Already throughout the book, Israel has sometimes obeyed, sometimes failed and repented. Those shortcomings not yet repented of—represented by the pockets of Canaanites and unclaimed land—still remain open to being addressed and rectified. At no point in the book of Joshua does Israel simply turn against YHWH and go its own way without looking back. It seems instead that the way in which the final redactor of the book presents Israel's situation under Joshua is encapsulated in the perpetual choice set before the people in 24:14–15. Perhaps more than at any other stage of its biblical story, Israel under Joshua constantly redirects its path toward YHWH when it errs. Given this portrait of Israel within the book, it seems more credible to read the statement in 21:43–45 as entirely sincere, when properly contextualized within the whole of the book and with the end of the Deuteronomistic History in view. Read this way, it both emphatically declares the full availability of all YHWH's promises to Israel, should Israel continue to choose to receive them in obedience, and safeguards YHWH's honor, aware that Israel will yet fail to inhabit fully all that YHWH has promised. Instead of conflicting voices, we are left with a picture of potential and actual realities, the story of the nation of Israel read in light of its end, yet always open to the possibility of Israel's present choice to acknowledge YHWH's call.

Joshua 24:11–13

The passage 24:11–13 lacks the emphatic tone of 21:43–45, instead treating the events of Israel's occupation of the land through YHWH's strength in a matter-of-fact way, as part of the history of YHWH's deeds on behalf of Israel. No remaining pockets of Canaanites and no incompleteness of occupation are mentioned or implied. Instead, YHWH's giving over of Israel's enemies and Israel's inheritance of the good and fruitful land thus made available serve as the central images of this text.[46] Perhaps the most notable feature of this text is that it is the only retrospective summary of the completed "conquest" and settlement in the book of Joshua presented in YHWH's own first-person speech, as conveyed by Joshua (24:2). In its context, it functions as part of the history that serves as the background, grounds, and motivation for Israel's ongoing choice of YHWH (24:14–24).[47]

Joshua 23:1, 3–5, 12–13: Rest and Unfinished Business

For the first time since their significant juxtaposition in chapters 11–12 and chapter 13, the two threads of the land theme meet again in chapter 23—and this time in a more conciliatory manner.[48] This meeting takes place in one of the great speeches of DtrH, a summary of Israel's experience of YHWH's actions in the distant and recent past, with implications for Israel's present and future.[49] Between the narrative framing and Joshua's first speech, the text presents us with a situation of rest from enemies, experienced in the presence of enemies. YHWH's work, as presented in Joshua's speech, is both past and future, both complete and ongoing: YHWH has brought about the downfall of the nations within Canaan (v. 4), but YHWH will continue to drive them out so that Israel can inherit their land (v. 5). YHWH has driven out the nations, and they have been unable to resist Him (v. 9). Yet the risk remains that Israel will form bonds with the remaining inhabitants of the land, thereby forfeiting YHWH's promise to drive them out and encountering YHWH's wrath (vv. 12–13). Here, the completed, successful work of YHWH in the past fuses with His ongoing advocacy of Israel to form the grounds for Israel's continued obedience. On the negative side, Joshua assures Israel that YHWH's curses are just as sure as His promises have thus far proved to be, should Israel stray from Him (vv. 14–16). In short, Israel dare not become complacent based on its past experience of good gifts from YHWH but must continue to serve Him in order to continue to experience His benefits.

The text of Joshua 23 seems to evince an integration of the strands of completeness and incompleteness within the land theme, pointing the reader to the two different messages conveyed by the different strands. It suggests that we are dealing not so much with conflicting data or even conflicting perspectives, as with different emphases within the land theme. In presenting the complex web of divine and human action involved in Israel's inheritance of the land, the book of Joshua alternately stresses different aspects of the scene presented, incorporating the varied emphases of its sources. The *integration* of these two contrasting strands in this passage following their previous prominent juxtaposition in chapters 11–13 suggests that the portrait of the taking of the land that the redacted text now presents is to be read primarily as multifaceted rather than as incoherent or discordant. The text does not dodge or dismiss either perspective but instead brings both together as true dimensions of the full picture.

Between "The Truth" and "The Whole Truth": YHWH Faithfully Gives, but Israel Must Actively Receive

The relationship between the divine description of incompleteness in chapter 13 and the statement of fulfillment at the end of chapter 11 follows a pattern of subversion that we have already seen enacted throughout the book. Things are not what they initially appear to be, whether because of explicit deception or undone expectations. The obedient conquest of Jericho turns out to be the scene of a hidden theft of consecrated goods. The delegation from "far away" with convincing evidence turns out to be the neighboring Gibeonites. The Canaanite prostitute who harbors the spies unexpectedly articulates a well-informed understanding of YHWH's plans for His chosen people. The altar built by the Transjordanian tribes is intended to serve as a sign of fidelity and unity among Israel instead of serving a competing cult. Again, in the case of Israel's reception of the land, the narrative takes a similar tack: what appears to be settled, done with, neatly wrapped up, is not simply so. According to the pattern that has been repeated so often in the book and will continue to be through its end, nothing is exactly what it seems to be or even what it is said to be, since more than one description comes together to form this composite portrait.

How should this pattern properly be described and explicated? What is happening in the text through these subversions, in terms of its effect on the reader? To put it negatively, we could say, as Hawk does, that the narrative undercuts itself, undermines its own portrayal of events; in this case, the text is self-subverting and self-deconstructing, taking apart what it brings together. We could follow Mitchell in speaking of conflicting sources that offer different visions of the "reality" of the conquest, perhaps one more "realistic" and another (or multiple others) less so. We could accept Polzin's argument that the text involves the subduing of one perspective by another. We could even argue that the combining and redaction of these accounts is purely accidental, that the pieces are simply scraps of stories found together and strung together chronologically any which way.

Each of these perspectives falls short by itself, in my view, failing to account sufficiently for either the origin or arrangement of the various pieces present in the text. Starting with the last notion, it seems nearly absurd to see the pieces in this text as haphazardly thrown together, given the common themes and patterns we have been describing. Too much regularity and consistency, too much *sense* in the ordering of the book's contents exists for the sequence *best* to be explained by accident. As for sources, we can indeed properly speak of different pieces and layers in the text; it is clearly not a unitary composition. But a description of the history of these sources cannot be summed up like an addition problem to describe the meaning of the present text composed of those parts.[50] In its final form, it may mean things and say things that none of its individual pieces ever did on their own. So the history of the text is only one ingredient in its meaning—we must still look for more. Finally, while it is appropriate to say that, in some sense, the text subverts its own portrayal of things, this is not the end of the story. Ultimately, it subverts itself with a *constructive* rather than deconstructive effect; rather than taking itself to pieces to turn sense into nonsense, the juxtaposition of the assembled pieces creates a *different* sense from any of the component parts of the text alone. The model of competing voices, which concludes that the text finds its meaning in a hierarchical ordering of perspectives, acknowledges this constructive conflict. Yet it does so by assuming that the relationship of differing voices in the text is conflictual because of their differences in content. I have argued, however, that we can take the multivocality of the text in an even more fruitful direction by recognizing the interaction of perspectives in the text as *conversational* and *expressive* rather than discordant and argumentative.

To borrow and adapt a phrase from Meir Sternberg, we might be able to speak of this as the text's move between "the truth" and "the whole truth," in the sense that the biblical text combines both explicit and implicit expression to convey its full meaning.[51] Chapter 11 states quite readily that Joshua "took all the land" (11:23), but attentive reading of this chapter and the following king lists shows that this "taking" (here, *lqḥ*) is portrayed in terms of the *conquest of kings,* not the *yrš*-ing—legal possession of[52]—territory. Through Joshua, YHWH broke the power of the rulers across the entire land of Canaan. Then chapter 13 fills us in on another dimension of the truth: in fact, significant parts of the *land* remain yet to be taken. In spite of the shattering of royal power, sections of the land are still held by Canaanites, even though this land too has been promised to Israel.[53] Not all of the land, then, is within Israel's control or presently available to be occupied by Israel. It is as if an apartment has been sold to a new party before the previous problem tenants have been evicted. But between the two, as noted above, we find the same affirmation: YHWH has kept, and will continue to keep, His promises to Israel; He will continue to act on behalf of Israel, both through Joshua while he lives, and in Israel's future, beyond Joshua's lifetime.

Yet another part of the "truth" comes out as the territory is divided. Israel has not succeeded in driving the Canaanites even from the cities that it has successfully settled. It seems that in some places, the Canaanites are simply too strong for them, and in one case, simply too imposing, despite Joshua's assertion that the Israelites are able to conquer even these well-equipped enemies. No reason for the persistence of these Canaanites is given in relation to YHWH, though the insistence in chapter 13 that YHWH Himself will finish dispossessing the Canaanites rings in the background. In terms of the text, they seem to function primarily as an ominous reminder of the warnings of Deuteronomy about the dangers of intermarriage, treaties, and worship with the people of the land. Apart from the Canaanites who possess iron chariots, most of these groups do not seem to present an active military threat—in fact, sometimes they are subdued by Israel, hinting at a tension between the two groups that sometimes breaks out into conflict, but which is balanced enough that neither group is strong enough to drive out the other. Even as the possibility and promise remain of YHWH's removal of the Canaanites within the land, they stand as a latent opportunity for disobedience, the option that remains for Israel to stray even when all is secure round about them and the land has rest from war. Settledness, they signal, cannot be mere complacency; Israel must continue to struggle with its identity vis-à-vis YHWH and the nations, continue to *choose* to serve, as Joshua's challenge at the end of the book makes clear.

Another significant function of the contingency opened up in Joshua 13 can be seen in relation to chapter 23. Joshua 23 offers a portrait of the conquest similar to that in chapter 13, speaking of the "allotment" of the "land that remains," and of the Lord "driving out" the inhabitants of it. This passage also shares with chapter 13 the aged Joshua (23:1) and an emphasis on YHWH's military actions on behalf of Israel (23:3). What it introduces into the open-ended conquest scheme outlined in chapter 13 is the possibility that Israel's own failure to heed the Lord's commands in their relationship with the inhabitants of the land will result in the Lord's ceasing to drive them out on Israel's behalf (23:12–13). At the same time, this concept of divine action contingent on Israel's obedience is not divorced from the surety of the divine promises portrayed at the end of chapter 21 and in chapter 11. Rather, 23:14–16 explicitly interlinks the two. It is, in fact, the reality and complete fulfillment of the "good promises" to Israel (v. 14) which guarantees the equal reality that the Lord will do all that He has sworn *against* Israel, should Israel stray after other gods (v. 16). Deliverance and destruction, life and death, are both equally part of the covenant promises. Israel must choose YHWH to choose life in the land.

Conclusion
Israel Did *Serve the Lord in the Book of Joshua*

Through the study of four major stories and a central theme, we have seen how the portrayal of Israel's obedient and disobedient actions in the book of Joshua all work in service of the claim that "Israel served the Lord during all the days of Joshua" (Josh 24:31). Even though several key actions of Israel in the book seem to challenge this summary statement, it in fact functions as a "hermeneutical key" by which to unlock one of the central points of these stories. By reading in this way, we encounter the spies' preservation of Rahab and her family not as a pragmatic, desperate, or sinful act, but as a proper response to her aiding of Israel and her acknowledgment of YHWH's works on behalf of His people. Not only does Rahab's action in harboring the spies demonstrate her faithfulness to Israel and Israel's God, but, as the spies declare to Joshua, it demonstrates above all YHWH's faithfulness to Israel in giving them the land: "Truly YHWH has given all the land into our hands" (2:24). When even an enemy aids in YHWH's and Israel's cause,

Israel cannot but see the hand of the Lord at work in its occupation of Canaan.

Likewise, while Achan's violation of the ḥerem appears at first to be a prime example of Israel's corporate sin, the outworking of the story serves to show instead Israel's willingness to seek out and destroy the sin in its midst. Even the potentially rebellious cry of Joshua—"Would that we had been content to settle beyond the Jordan!" (7:7)—is channeled here into an appeal to YHWH's character. Joshua is not simply expressing dissent, but instead responding openly to YHWH's apparent failure to keep His promise to be present with Israel in battle. Thus he asks what the consequences will be for YHWH's reputation among the nations if He allows His people to be destroyed: "Then what will you do for your great name?" (7:9). In response, YHWH clarifies that the failure to keep faith lies with Israel, not Himself, and graciously provides Israel with a way of returning to His favor. Israel, in return, faithfully follows YHWH's instructions and roots out the sin of Achan and the ḥerem in its midst. An incident that could have been a disaster for all Israel or could have devolved into an exchange of accusations with YHWH instead provides Israel with a second chance at faithfulness, which Israel accepts. By showing this, the story illustrates that among fallible human beings, true faithfulness to the Lord is not found exclusively in flawless obedience, but also in the proper response to sin.

Israel has another opportunity to demonstrate this pattern of inadvertent sin and the subsequent search for an appropriate response in the case of the Gibeonites. This time, YHWH is silent, perhaps partly because Israel does not inquire of Him, failing to "ask direction from the Lord" (9:14) before sealing a treaty with the supposed supplicants from afar. Yet Israel reasons through the situation in a way that demonstrates its knowledge of the Deuteronomic Law, and thus the implicit presence of the book of the Torah as the guide for Israel's actions. This becomes apparent to the reader from Israel's question, "Perhaps you live among us; then how can we make a treaty with you?" (9:7), evoking the Deuteronomic prohibitions on treaties with the Canaanites. Even though the text does not use the word ḥerem to speak of the people's intention to attack the Gibeonites, the two competing obligations are clearly in view: does the command to subject the Canaanites to destruction take priority, or the oath made before YHWH in contracting a treaty with them? The leaders of Israel opt for the latter in declaring, "We have sworn to them by YHWH, the God of Israel, and now we must not touch them" (9:19), putting the sanctity of an oath by the divine name before the *ḥerem* command. Yet at the same time, Joshua symbolically submits the Gibeonites to the *ḥerem* in committing them to the service of the "house of God" (9:22–23), devoting them as a living offering to YHWH, whose works they have acknowledged in their deception and by whose name they are inseparably bound to Israel. That Israel has chosen rightly in prioritizing the oath and preserving the lives of the Gibeonites is shown by the lack of reprisal by YHWH after the incident, as is also true in the case of Rahab. Israel continues to enjoy the benefits of YHWH's advocacy in battle—including the battle in defense of Gibeon.

Last among Israel's moral dilemmas is the case of the Transjordanian altar, showing that challenges to Israel's faithfulness continue to arise even in the absence of opposition from the Canaanites. Despite the threats from enemies, it is actually Israel's own decisions for obedience or disobedience that most significantly chart its course in the land. Other nations have no power against Israel when YHWH acts on Israel's behalf, but Israel itself can jeopardize this divine advocacy by its failure to serve YHWH. The story of the Transjordanian altar demonstrates the need for Israel's continuing vigilance against sin, but also the need for careful consideration in cases of possible violation. As in the story of the Gibeonites, YHWH remains silent throughout the episode, but the question of a noncentral altar built for unclear purposes again evokes the concerns of the book of Deuteronomy that worship of YHWH be conducted properly and in the proper place. Instead of falling into sin by acting too hastily once more, as they did in the treaty with Gibeon, the Cisjordanians who are suspicious of their brothers across the river send a commission to investigate the questionable altar. Through discussion and explanation, the concerns of both parties are expressed and alleviated, so that neither group ends in sin against the other, whether by too quick reprisal or by straying into the worship of other gods. Once more, the story is brought under the rubric of "Israel served the Lord," uniting Israel in mutual understanding and proper worship even as it is divided by the Jordan.

Finally, Israel's overall pattern of partial occupation of the land by the conclusion of the book once more raises initial doubts in the reader that the verdict will be sustained. But in the book of Joshua, the patchwork of occupied and yet-to-be-occupied territories points to the unfinished task of Israel's obedience and the ongoing work of YHWH in giving Israel the land rather than indicating Israel's failure. The contrast between the use of the "incomplete occupation" motif here and in the beginning of the book of Judges shows that it does not function in Joshua for Israel's condemnation, as it will after Joshua has passed away and Israel opts to live among Canaanites rather than subdue them. Instead, it shows how the relationship between the Lord and Israel, between YHWH's advocacy and Israel's obedience, has not ended even once Israel has entered the land. The gift of the land is not a static grant, but a gift that exists only in dynamic relation to YHWH's giving. That giving, at least, the book of Joshua assures Israel, is reliable and perfect, as 21:43–45 shows. Israel, however, must continue to *receive* the land from YHWH, in a two-way transaction that requires Israel's action in response to YHWH's giving. It is this process, depicted especially in the latter part of the book of Joshua, that falls apart in the first few chapters of Judges, as Israel ceases to receive YHWH's gift of the land actively and lapses into complacency. By its slippage into commingling with the Canaanite inhabitants of the cities during the period of the judges, Israel chooses the path that leads away from YHWH's will and YHWH's gift of the land, and instead brings it dangerously into the territory of YHWH's warnings of judgment in Deuteronomy 7:1–4 and 12:28–32. Yet within the book of Joshua, the two paths remain before Israel as real possibilities: the continued occupation of the land that YHWH has given and will keep giving into Israel's hands, or the neglect and eventual loss of that gift through fearfulness and apathy. Thus, even amidst indications of the incomplete taking of the land in Joshua, the book sustains an air of hopefulness that Israel may indeed choose the former path and live long in the land the Lord has given.

Cumulatively, these texts from Joshua show that the Deuteronomistic concept of obedience is not merely an artificial ideal that Israel always fails to achieve, but rather a reality that is worked out in the messy vicissitudes of Israel's history. Israel's attempts to mirror YHWH's holiness indeed end up littered with ambiguities, errors, and outright failures. Yet even in the midst of this, Israel's earnest pursuit of obedience meets with YHWH's approval and counts as true service of the Lord. It is true, as Joshua says, that Israel "cannot serve YHWH, for He is a holy God" (24:19). He is a jealous God, Joshua warns, and will not forgive Israel's transgressions (v. 19). At the same time, though, Israel *does* choose to serve YHWH during Joshua's days, and YHWH has chosen Israel, imperfect as it is, to be His own "treasured possession"— a relationship that not even Israel's most blatant iniquities can sever.

Contrary to Nelson's claim, then, Joshua does not stand in kingly (dis)guise as the heroic center of the book that bears his name. Mitchell's analysis also falls short in its discovery in the book of Joshua of an implicit antipathy toward "outsiders," when Rahab and the Gibeonites find a haven—and even blessing!—by their association with Israel. Similarly, Hawk's reading of the book errs even further on the side of negativity, judging Israel to be rife with corruption under Joshua, and thus requires an ironic reading of many of the positive claims of the book. Polzin's linking of the simultaneous occupation of Law and land comes closest to conveying the spirit of the narrative sequence, but his identification of the voices of the text as competitive rather than conversational does not succeed in understanding the book as an integrated and coherent textual whole.

In this way, the present work makes a distinctive contribution to the study of the book of Joshua by taking the text's concluding verdict that "Israel served the Lord all the days of Joshua" as an earnest evaluation, essential to what the book as a whole communicates—more than a mere accident of redaction or compilation. When taken seriously as an integral part of the text's meaning, this claim is so strong and surprising that it must be brought into conversation with the book's contents and given a chance to substantiate its claim. As we have seen, the adoption of this verse as a "hermeneutical key," given its summary evaluation of the generation under Joshua, brings out a previously overlooked significance in the stories of the initial era of Israel's settlement in the land. They do not serve simply as a historical record of Israel's past, or merely as an account of Israel's uneven success in obeying YHWH's commands in the course of occupying the land. Instead, the book of Joshua presents stories and commentary about Israel's early days in the land, carefully selected and arranged, in a way that creates a complex portrait of what it means for Israel to serve YHWH—a portrait that it makes available to future generations of Israel as well.

The portrait that this book presents to the reader is a portrait of hope. Israel under Joshua is, in some sense, an ideal generation, a model for later readers of their forays into the land of promise. The generation under Joshua lacks the rebellious spirit that doomed the wilderness generation that preceded and sired it; likewise, it avoids the laissez-faire attitude of the generations under the judges, which treat YHWH as little more than a rescuer who can be counted on to bail out His people when they fall to foreign oppressors as a consequence of their sin. Instead, the generation under Joshua seeks to serve and obey the Lord, entering the land in serene obedience, keeping the commanded observances that had been neglected, and carefully following the peculiar divine instructions for the conquest of Jericho. Yet as the texts that we have examined have shown, Israel's obedience under Joshua could hardly be called flawless. By depicting Israel's true service to YHWH as consisting in striving toward obedience and repenting when it falls short, the Deuteronomistic writers encourage an Israelite audience that errs and must face the consequences of its errors. Israel's attempts at obedience under Joshua's leadership show that the sequence of repentance, forgiveness, and restoration has been a part of Israel's life before YHWH from the beginning of its time in the land. The model generation does not serve as a model of perfection, but as a model of striving toward obedience and attunement to YHWH's will. Like the generation under Joshua, Israel may sometimes be guided by an immediate word from the Lord and sometimes by His Torah. In either case, YHWH's revelation of His character and His plans for Israel is always available to His chosen people throughout their generations. Israel need only turn toward YHWH in a wholehearted effort to serve Him, and YHWH, in His mercy and covenant love, will make up what Israel lacks, because, knowing all of Israel's foibles and fallibilities, YHWH has chosen Israel from among all the nations of the earth to be in relationship with Him, so that Israel, in spite of all its imperfections, can truly say, "I am my beloved's, and his desire is for me" (Song 7:10).

Notes

Introduction: The Fragmentation of the Book of Joshua

1. Von Rad, "Problem of the Hexateuch," 1–78.

2. These approaches to Joshua are often reflected in the older introductions to the Old Testament; see, for example, Driver, *Introduction to the Old Testament*, 104; Pfeiffer, *Introduction*; and Fohrer and Eissfeldt below.

3. In relation to Joshua in particular, see Albright, "The Israelite Conquest," 11–22. Contrast this with the strongly deductive textual approach of Alt, "The Settlement of the Israelites," 173–21.

4. For a concise summary of the disputes over the interpretation of Jericho and a new proposal—which itself has been disputed—see Wood, "Did the Israelites Conquer Jericho?," 44–58.

5. Childs, *Biblical Theology*, 98.

6. Walter Brueggemann talks about Old Testament theology in terms of "testimony" but in a rather different sense from Brevard Childs's "witness." For Brueggemann, this "testimony" is one position argued for among other accounts of reality. See his application of this perspective to the book of Joshua in his brief monograph *Divine Presence amid Violence*.

7. Steven McKenzie critiques Rudolf Smend's theory of DtrH put forward in "Die Gesetz und die Völker," 494–509, on the basis that the muddled text of Joshua is shaky ground on which to found such an edifice (McKenzie, "Deuteronomistic History," n.p.).

8. Noth, *Deuteronomistic History*, 36.

9. For example, Noth says that Dtr essentially writes his own version of the Caleb story, oriented toward his particular purposes, based on traditional materials he wishes to include in some form or other (*Deuteronomistic History*, 39).

10. Noth, *Deuteronomistic History*, 5, 36.

11. Noth, *Deuteronomistic History*, 40. He bases this conclusion on the identity of 13:1a with 23:1b, as well as the earlier statement of the division of the land and the completion of the conquest in 11:23.

12. Noth, *Deuteronomistic History*, 8.

13. Gressmann, *Die Schriften*, 14, as cited by Childs in "The Etiological Tale," 387–97.

14. Following in the footsteps of Hermann Gunkel's pioneering description of etiological legends (*Genesis*, xviii).

15. Scholars have puzzled over the precise meaning of this phrase for some time. See, for example, Childs, "'Until This Day,'" 279–92, and more recently, Geoghegan, *The Evidence of "Until This Day."*

16. Childs, "'Until This Day,'" 279–92.

17. Other studies dealing with smaller sections within the book have been composed as well, but these are less immediately relevant to our goal of finding a method for reading the book in its entirety as a literary unit. See, for example, Rowlett's fascinating and well-crafted study, which deals only with the first nine chapters, *Joshua and the Rhetoric of Violence*. Although I disagree with her conclusions on the whole, I find her methodology potentially quite fruitful.

18. See Polzin, *Moses and the Deuteronomist*, 1–24, for the introduction of this concept that the Dtr texts find their meaning in a dialogue between narratorial and quoted speech rather than expressing "a single dominating point of view which subordinates all others in the work." He develops the details of this concept particularly in the major Mosaic speeches of Deuteronomy, identifying two conflicting voices of unequal weight whose dispute conveys the book's theological perspective (Polzin, *Moses and the Deuteronomist*, 25–72). According to Polzin, this discursive expression of a Dtr perspective pervades the whole of DtrH, including the book of Joshua.

19. Gunn, "Joshua-Judges," 110.

20. Hawk, *Every Promise Fulfilled*.

21. Mitchell, *Together in the Land*.

Chapter 1. "Israel Served the Lord": A Hermeneutical Key

1. A "verdict" that correlates with Dtr's setting up of the generation under Joshua as a positive foil for the next generation, "who neither knew the

Lord nor what He had done for Israel" (Jdg 2:10) in the time of the judges. Note that all translations of biblical passages are my own, or are my own adaptations unless otherwise noted.

2. See below for a discussion of the Deuteronomic laws in relation to the book of Joshua.

3. This title is evocative of Joshua's own faithfulness in terms of following in the footsteps of "the servant of the Lord," a title frequently employed with reference to Moses in the book of Joshua (Josh 1:1, 2, 7, 13, 15). Joshua begins the book, on the other hand, as "the assistant of Moses" (Josh 1:1), and only at the conclusion of the book is honored with the title that belonged to Moses at the beginning (Josh 24:29).

4. For example, see Nelson, *Joshua,* 279, and Butler, *Joshua,* 283.

5. See Deuteronomy 7:1-6 and 20:16-18 on the eradication of the nations of the land before Israel as it takes the land; especially Deut 7:2 and 20:17 imply the complete devotion of the nations to YHWH by destruction by their use of the term *ḥerem*. On the *ḥerem* command, see the excursus in chapter 3. See also Mitchell, *Together in the Land,* 52-66, for a discussion of *ḥerem* particularly in relation to the story of Jericho and Achan, but with a useful broader summary of the term's range of usage.

6. Stated in Joshua 13:13, 15:63, 16:10, 17:12-13, and implied in 19:47. In addition, YHWH mentions in 13:6-7 that He Himself will be responsible for driving out the people of the northern mountain regions, whose land is meanwhile to be allotted nonetheless.

7. Some see the statement as intended to establish a contrast between the days of Joshua and the period of the judges; see, for example, Gray, *Joshua,* 196; Mitchell, *Together in the Land,* 147-48; and Nelson, *Joshua,* 280.

8. For example, Creach's commentary seems to miss the verse for this reason.

9. Gray, *Joshua,* 196-97; Mitchell, *Together in the Land,* 147-48; Nelson, *Joshua,* 280.

10. Scholars differ in their opinion of the precise relationship between these two verses, in terms of their sequence of composition. Noth suggests that the Judges passage is secondarily incorporated into Joshua to provide a sense of closure once the originally joined books are broken apart (Noth, *Deuteronomistic History,* 102). Similarly, Gray takes the passage in Judges as a resumptive device that accommodates the insertion of Judges 1:1-2:5 into the second edition of DtrH (Gray, *Joshua,* 244); Soggin reaches a similar conclusion, regarding the insertion of this passage and the end of Joshua 24 (Soggin, *Joshua,* 245). Butler assigns priority to the passage in Joshua, which Judges subsequently "takes up" (Butler, *Joshua,* 283; though cf. his discussion on p. 281, in which the order of composition is less clear). Mitchell takes *both* verses to be

"subsequent compositional elements" inserted to link the books to one another (Mitchell, *Together in the Land,* 148). Woudstra, on the other hand, takes the parallel passages as a sign of the canonical unity of the two books, emphasizing the "interlinking" of the books rather than the sequence of composition (Woudstra, *Joshua,* 359).

11. Hawk, *Every Promise,* 139 (but with a caveat); Noth, *Deuteronomistic History,* 102; Mitchell, *Together in the Land,* 147–48; Butler, *Joshua,* 283; Hoppe, *Joshua,* 100; Woudstra, *Joshua,* 360.

12. Butler, *Joshua,* 283.

13. Hoppe, *Joshua,* 100.

14. Woudstra, *Joshua,* 360.

15. It should be noted that this label is not meant to describe *all* historically subsequent additions to the text that might be called "glosses" or "redactions." It is meant only to encompass statements that make sweeping claims for or judgments on a person, action, or era which seem to require the text to be read in a different light. Here, my approach closely resembles the canonical approach of Brevard Childs, who sees the shaping of the biblical text by its redactors and transmitters as providing hermeneutical guidance for future readers (Childs, *Biblical Theology of the Old and New Testaments,* 71).

16. Mitchell also reads the book of Joshua in terms of the "juxtaposition of contrasting ideas" (Mitchell, *Together in the Land,* 188), but particularly in relation to remnants of the nations remaining in the land in contrast to Israel's command to subject them to ḥerem.

17. Judges 2 indeed develops this idea further, repeating the report of Joshua's passing (vv. 8–9), but this time unfolding its implications for the subsequent behavior of Israel in contrast to the generation that entered the land (vv. 10–15).

18. Robert Alter makes a similar point, understanding contradictions as actively functioning to introduce complications into a narrative rather resulting from the work of a "naive" redactor who fails to recognize these contradictions as such (Alter, *Art of Biblical Narrative,* 138).

19. Some readers may also question the value of selecting such a "key" from within the text itself rather than from another source. Every redactor or reader who approaches the text will inevitably bring *something* to the text in his or her interpretation of it, whether for good or ill. Certain readers will choose, however, to focus their reading on a particular center, their "hermeneutical key" for understanding the text, whether political interests, issues of gender, or religious beliefs. These readers approach the text with an acknowledged purpose and agenda that makes the reader the primary agent of the text's meaning. In my view, the value of seeking a means of "sense-making" within the text is that it grants the text as much integrity as a dialogue-partner

as possible, making an effort to approach the text on its own terms. While the reader's choice of a "key" may still reflect the influence of his or her own experience, knowledge, and beliefs, it demonstrates a good faith effort to permit the text to have a separate voice, enabling true interaction with the text rather than reducing it to a mouthpiece for the reader's views. See Sternberg, *Poetics of Biblical Narrative*, 186–90 (esp. 188), for a good discussion of "illegitimate gap-filling" that resonates somewhat with my view.

20. Compare Mikhail M. Bakhtin's seminal exploration of polyphony as a means of truth-telling in *Problems of Dostoyevsky's Poetics*.

21. Brevard Childs speaks of this integration of the redactional elements with the source materials as part of the "canonical shaping" of the text, an intentional interpretational process that has taken place in the process of the text's transmission by communities of faith "in order to provide means for its continuing appropriation by its subsequent hearers" (*Biblical Theology*, 71, 73).

22. Polzin, *Moses and the Deuteronomist*, 152–53.

23. Joshua 1:6, 7, 9; echoed by the Transjordanian tribes in 1:18.

24. This is reflected also in that when the Transjordanians repeat the Lord's charge back to Joshua, it follows immediately upon their declaration that Joshua's words and commands must be obeyed (1:18) in a manner parallel to Moses' (1:17). Obedience to Joshua is placed in the context of the Lord's continued presence with Joshua, a presence that presumably depends on Joshua's continuing faithfulness to the Lord—i.e., "strong and courageous" obedience in claiming the gift of the land.

25. The aftermath of the treaty with the Gibeonites is a particularly notable example of this lack of divine speech or action—even lack of condemnation—where we might expect it. See below for a closer examination of the account of the treaty with the Gibeonites.

26. Note, for example, that the covenant ceremony of Joshua 8:30–35 mentions the book of the Law twice more (vv. 31, 34), immediately preceding Israel's inadvertent, if incautious, violation of the command not to make treaties with the inhabitants of the land.

27. Polzin, *Moses and the Deuteronomist*, 152–53.

28. Deuteronomy 12:4–14, 26–27, twice states the necessity of a single Israelite worship site, but places the main emphasis on centralized *sacrifice*, without any specific prohibition on the building of other altars that are not used for sacrifice. While Deuteronomy 12:2–3 requires the destruction of pagan altars, nothing is directly said about the peculiar possibility of nonsacrificial Israelite altars. The Transjordanian altar may fall into the legal loophole of the unexpected exception.

29. Historically speaking, it is possible that this tension could point toward the theory proposed by Jon Levenson regarding the later insertion of the

book of the Torah in the book of Deuteronomy (Levenson, "Who Inserted the Book of the Torah?," 203–33). The fact that significant stories in the book of Joshua grate against Deuteronomic norms suggests that those norms may have been absent from the Dtr corpus at the time of Dtr's first redaction of Joshua.

Chapter 2. The Stories of Rahab and Achan

1. For example, the following scholars contrast the fates of Rahab and Achan in a variety of ways: Mitchell, *Together in the Land*, 81–82; Nelson, *Joshua*, 19–20; and Rowlett, *Rhetoric of Violence*, 176–79.

2. Creach, *Joshua*, 31.

3. The history of Christian interpretation of this passage offers a few examples of censure of Rahab's lie, but these are mitigated by the frequent conclusion that Rahab's deception is forgiven as a response of divine mercy for her kindness to the spies. For a discussion of Augustine's comments on this point, see Kritzinger, "Rahab, illa meretrix," 28; for John Calvin's ruminations on the ethics of Rahab's lie and treason, see *Commentary on Joshua*, 2:4. Many more interpreters, however, offer praise for her action and/or for her figurative meaning. For a consideration of Rahab's treatment in the early Christian writings, see Stander, "The Greek Church Fathers and Rahab," 37–49; and Kritzinger, "Rahab, illa meretrix," 22–36, who discusses her depiction in the Latin Church Fathers.

4. See Cohen, "Rahab," 17:66–67, for a discussion of attempts to understand the Targumic translation of *zônâ* as "innkeeper."

5. For a discussion of rabbinic interpretations of Rahab, see Bronner, *From Eve to Esther*, 147–51; and Beek, "Jewish Exegesis," 37–44, which is useful primarily for the rabbinic references it contains.

6. See Bronner, *From Eve to Esther*, 149n22, and Beek, "Jewish Exegesis," for rabbinic references.

7. Yair Zakovitch offers a folkloric reading in "Humor and Theology," 73–98.

8. See Campbell, "Rahab's Covenant," 243–44.

9. E.g., see Creach, *Joshua*, 32–33, who finds "clear allusions to sexual activity" and sees sexual innuendo as "a driving force in [the story's] plot"; and Hawk, *Every Promise*, 61–62, who finds "strong sexual overtones" in the verbs that link the spies with Rahab.

10. Spina, *Faith of the Outsider*, 57, takes the oath to be a "direct violation of God's Torah"; Hawk, *Joshua*, 46, terms it a "flagrant violation" of Deuteronomy 7 in particular; and Boling and Wright, *Joshua*, 150, pointing instead to the *ḥerem* formulation in Deuteronomy 20, describe the relationship between

the oath and Deuteronomy 20:10–20 as a "glaring internal contradiction." Nelson, *Joshua,* 46, speaks more mildly of tension between the two texts, and Creach, *Joshua,* 31, sees the story as anticipating that the *ḥerem* decree will be more complicated to execute than it may seem.

Interestingly, the perception of conflict between these two texts does not necessarily entail a negative assessment of Rahab or the story overall in these commentators; only Hawk perceives an ominous shadow hovering over the entire encounter, even while recognizing Rahab's effective incorporation into Israel by the end of the story (Hawk, *Joshua,* 50). Polzin offers the most original reading of the story by taking it in a figurative direction; in reading Rahab as a type of Israel, he understands the oath as a "merciful application of the Law" parallel to what Israel itself has experienced from YHWH (Polzin, *Moses and the Deuteronomist,* 113–14).

11. Surprisingly, many commentators do not even remark on the presence of the oath, concerned more with precisely identifying Rahab's profession and the spies' occasion for entering her house, attempting to clear the spies of charges of soliciting a prostitute while leaving them open to the much more serious charge of making covenants with Canaanites!

12. It seems that Rahab's boldness and tenacity in demanding an oath on the basis of her *ḥesed* could be understood in quite a different light; compare Jacob's refusal to stop wrestling with the divine being until he receives a blessing in Genesis 32:26. This similarity may augment Polzin's argument that Rahab serves as a type of Israel (for his full analysis of the story, see Polzin, *Moses and the Deuteronomist,* 85–91).

13. Hawk, *Joshua,* 41.

14. Hawk, *Every Promise,* 68–69.

15. Hawk, *Joshua,* 46.

16. Only the particular practices of prostitution labeled as *qĕdēšā* and *qādēš,* whose precise nature remains uncertain, are specifically banned under Deuteronomic law in Deuteronomy 23:18. Apart from this, a number of laws assume the possibility of the practice of prostitution, including Leviticus 19:29, which restricts a man from offering his daughter as a prostitute; Leviticus 21:7, which forbids a priest to marry a women engaged in prostitution; and Deuteronomy 23:18, which bans the payment of vows with proceeds from prostitution.

17. Soggin, *Joshua,* 39.

18. Bronner, *From Eve to Esther,* 149n21.

19. Cross, "Response to Yair Zakovitch," 103n3.

20. On this subject, see van der Toorn's article "Female Prostitution," 193–205, where the author presents an interesting study that is unfortunately skewed by the notion that Israelite religion generally disenfranchised women.

21. Gottwald, *Tribes of [YHWH]*, 557.

22. Boling and Wright laudably acknowledge the humor of the story (Boling and Wright, *Joshua*, 147), a feature neglected by most commentators apart from broad sexual references; Zakovitch appreciates this dimension as well but overplays it (Zakovitch, "Humor and Theology," 75–98). In contrast, see Hawk, whose commentary on Joshua and his literary study of the book both find this account to be permeated with ominous overtones (Hawk, *Joshua* and *Every Promise*).

23. Calvin, incidentally, is concerned to justify her act of treason against her countrymen in harboring the spies, which he achieves to his own satisfaction in the end (Calvin, *Joshua*, online).

24. MacDonald, *Monotheism*, 195. Although he does not discuss the Joshua 2:11 passage in detail, I credit his discussion of this phrase with drawing this linkage to my attention.

25. MacDonald, *Monotheism*, 195.

26. See particularly 4:35–36, where the voice and the fire are distinguished as the heavenly and earthly elements of YHWH's theophany at Horeb.

27. MacDonald, *Monotheism*, 195–96.

28. Levenson's essay "From Temple to Synagogue," 143–66, further advances our analysis of this passage by identifying several key features of Solomon's prayer in 1 Kings 8:23–53 as "distinctly exilic." On the basis of specific verbal and theological features—including the phrase describing YHWH as "God in heaven above and on earth below," whose only close parallels he finds in Deuteronomy 4:39 and Joshua 2:11—he convincingly attributes this passage to Dtr^2 (Levenson, "From Temple to Synagogue," 160). Conversely, we can argue that Rahab's speech in Joshua 2:11 can credibly be attributed to Dtr^2 as well.

29. See Creach, *Joshua*, 1, for a similar perspective on the role of the Law in the book.

30. E.g., Deuteronomy 7:12, 8:18, with *bĕrît* as the object of the verb.

31. E.g., Deuteronomy 6:13, "Fear the Lord your God, serve Him only, and take your oaths in His name"; Joshua 14:9, Moses' oath that Israel will receive the land.

32. For example, see the oath that Abraham makes his servant swear regarding the choice of Isaac's wife (Gen 24:1–4), Saul's oath to Jonathan that he will not kill David (1 Sam 19:6), and David's oath to Bathsheba that Solomon will be king (1 Kgs 1:29–30).

33. Polzin, *Moses and the Deuteronomist*, chapter 3. This might be true, if we identify Dtr as the compiler of the Joshua stories—a conclusion that goes against Noth's analysis that this "chain" preexisted the Dtr form of the book. If

not, we should consider the possibility that Polzin has read the situation backward; if the *ḥerem* language has largely been "imposed" on the chain of stories adopted into the book of Joshua texts by the Dtr redactor, then perhaps we would do better to speak instead of the *ḥerem* language as an exegesis of the story of Israel's occupation of the land!

34. See Mitchell, *Together in the Land*, 81–82, for discussion of additional contrasting correspondences between the two stories.

35. That the spies do not conceal their oath as Hawk accuses is demonstrated by Joshua's knowledge of it in 6:22, where he affirms the oath by commanding its fulfillment.

36. Creach, *Joshua*, 17; Spina, *Faith of the Outsider*, 58–61.

37. Boling and Wright, *Joshua*, 147; Hawk, *Joshua*, 46.

38. Campbell, "Rahab's Covenant," 243–44. On the other hand, Campbell's argument for Rahab's familiarity with the covenant form because her profession of "barmaid" makes her privy to the royal court seems a highly dubious historical back-construction, likely based on Mesopotamian laws relating to the responsibilities of tavern-keepers to report treason plotted in their hearing (though Campbell does not provide his sources). Rather, any reflection of the covenant form is far more likely the work of a Dtr hand.

39. Note that Ruth's declaration to Naomi that "your God will be my God" (Ruth 1:16), recalling Rahab in her boldness and sheer force of will, still requires Naomi to accept Ruth's company on the trip to Israel; Ruth cannot "make herself" an Israelite.

40. If early Israel's group boundaries are defined primarily in terms other than common ancestry (though this clearly has an important place in Israel's self-conception) or national identity, some permeability of these boundaries seems possible. For recent discussions of ethnicity in ancient Israel, see Miller, "Identifying Earliest Israel," 55–68, who asserts that "ethnologists have long given up any notion that equates ethnicity with genealogical affiliation"; and Bloch-Smith, "Israelite Ethnicity in Iron I," 401–25, esp. 402–5, where she proposes a definition of early Israel based primarily on "shared interests" rather than shared descent (Bloch-Smith, "Israelite Ethnicity in Iron I," 405).

41. Kaminsky, *Yet I Loved Jacob*, 121–36.

42. Kaminsky, *Yet I Loved Jacob*, 111–20.

43. Kaminsky, *Yet I Loved Jacob*, 111.

44. This anti-elect action can, of course, be reinforced and directed by YHWH for His own purposes; see, for example, the hardening of Pharaoh's heart for the demonstration of YHWH's power (Exod 7:1–5, 9:13–16), and the Canaanites' bellicosity as the means of their obliteration by YHWH (Josh 11:20).

45. Mitchell, *Together in the Land*, 148, observes that Rahab is the exception to the contrast between the nations "hearing" and "fearing," and Israel "seeing" and "knowing" in the book of Joshua (see Mitchell, *Together in the Land*, 142–51, for his discussion of this pattern).

46. Both Rahab and Ruth act on their own initiative to participate in Israel and acknowledge YHWH as God (Josh 2:11; Ruth 1:16), without invitation—in Ruth's case, in spite of active discouragement (Ruth 1:8, 11)! Yet each ultimately benefits from her decision and action, however audaciously undertaken.

47. Nelson, *Joshua*, 50.

48. Creach, *Joshua*, 36–37.

49. Divided rabbinic opinion on this matter is described by Rabinowitz and Eichhorn, "Proselytes," 16:587–94. Rabinowitz writes that, according to certain authorities, "the proselyte, praying by himself, must say: 'the God of the Fathers of Israel'; in the synagogue he says: 'the God of your Fathers' (Ma'as. Sh. 5:14; Bik. 1:4)" (Rabinowitz and Eichhorn, "Proselytes," 588). These rabbis opt for the same style of self-distancing that we observed above in the case of Rahab. Eichhorn, on the other hand, notes that R. Samson and Maimonides permitted the proselyte to say "the God of Our Fathers," on the basis "that Abraham was the father of the whole world" (Rabinowitz and Eichhorn, "Proselytes," 588).

50. Milgrom, "Religious Conversion," 169–76.

51. Gottwald, *Tribes of [YHWH]*, 556–63. Note, however, that he describes this "conversion" as incorporation into "the burgeoning alternative social system of Israel," not an Israelite "religion," thereby defining conversion in a social rather than a religious sense (556).

52. Gottwald, *Tribes of [YHWH]*, 556–58.

53. Milgrom, "Religious Conversion," 169–75.

54. Milgrom, "Religious Conversion," 175.

55. Milgrom, "Religious Conversion," 172.

56. Gottwald's response to Milgrom shows that Milgrom and he are talking past each other at a much more fundamental level than perhaps either realizes. This is best captured by Gottwald's own description of his project as "sociological demythologization of YHWHistic faith" (Gottwald, *Tribes of [YHWH]*, 708). For example, Gottwald presents a persistently *social* understanding of what he means by "conversion," reflected in his portrayal of Milgrom's objections as opposition to the "hypothesis that Israel originated by means of a social revolution," with no direct reference to its religious dimension (Gottwald, "Religious Conversion," 49). The fact that Gottwald can use the phrase "recruitment of membership" as the equivalent of the phrase "religious conversion" (Gottwald, "Religious Conversion," 50) suggests that Gottwald is

not actually talking about "mass conversions" to Israel's "covenantal faith" in the sense that Milgrom supposes (Milgrom, "Religious Conversion," 175).

57. I employ the phrase *religious system* here to indicate the full spectrum of religious beliefs and practices undertaken by a given religion, thereby avoiding the reductionism that can be implied by the terms *faith* or *cult* alone.

58. Milgrom, "Religious Conversion," 175.

59. This also coheres with the outcome of the Gibeonite treaty, where Joshua guides the Israelites to choose the preservation of their treaty-partners' lives as menial laborers devoted to YHWH's sanctuary rather than carrying out the prior command of ḥerem. While the order of events is different, the dynamic at work in each text is similar.

60. Contrary to Hawk's implication that the spies concealed their oath to Rahab, based on the brief report they make to Joshua in 2:24 (Hawk, *Every Promise*, 70–71), the previous verse indicates that the spies in fact recount everything that had befallen them, and verse 24 serves only as the summary or conclusion of their report.

61. Polzin reads Rahab as a "type" of Israel, in fact, as noted above (Polzin, *Moses and the Deuteronomist*, 85–91; esp. 88 and 90); while I do not find his reading convincing in every detail, his comparison is quite illuminating.

62. Butler, *Joshua*, 80, similarly reads it specifically as an example of "how to deal with divine anger."

63. Once in the narrator's voice, in Joshua 7:1, and once in the Lord's speech to Joshua, in 7:11, the violation is stated—notably, both references attribute the transgression to Israel as a whole.

64. Achan's in Joshua 7:1, 15, 20; Israel's also in 7:1, and in 7:11.

65. Polzin's claim that the text attributes the defeat at Ai partly to Joshua's sending of the spies in Joshua 2 in addition to Achan's theft is unfounded (Polzin, *Moses and the Deuteronomist*, 114). What seems more interesting is the similarity between the sending of spies in the case of Ai and that of Jericho, contrasted with the remarkably different outcomes of the two campaigns.

66. Mitchell, *Together in the Land*, 146.

67. Joshua 2:24; 6:2; 8:1, 18; 10:8, 19, 32; 11:8; 21:44; 24:8, 11.

68. The occasions for these complaints are as follows: Exodus 14:11–12, the sight of the pursuing Egyptians; Exodus 17:3, in response to lack of water; and Numbers 14:2–3, the spies' report regarding land, which Deuteronomy 1:27 recalls.

69. Mitchell's negative assessment of Joshua's complaint in Joshua 7:7 on the basis that its content is "almost identical" to that of the Israelites' grumbling in Deuteronomy 1:27 fails to account for a crucial difference between the two incidents (Mitchell, *Together in the Land*, 68): While the Israelites grumble about YHWH's action among themselves, in the privacy of their own tents in

Deuteronomy 1:27—"behind YHWH's back," so to speak—Joshua addresses his complaint directly to YHWH.

70. Butler, *Joshua*, 79–80; Nelson, *Joshua*, 104.

71. Butler, *Joshua*, 80.

72. A situation that would obtain if YHWH turned out to be a "loose cannon," as Walter Brueggemann colorfully suggests (Brueggemann, *Theology of the Old Testament*, 296).

73. This appeal recalls Moses' mediation on behalf of Israel in Exodus 32:12 and Numbers 14:13–16, drawing an implicit parallel between Joshua's and Moses' roles. Hawk's conclusion that this comparison is ironic, with Joshua as "a virtual antitype of Moses" (Hawk, *Every Promise*, 76–77), seems to give Joshua's attempt insufficient credit. YHWH's rebuke is directed toward the purpose of Israel's restoration, not the dismissal of Joshua's mediation, since it is only through Joshua's intercession that YHWH provides Israel with a way to mitigate His own wrath. Nelson also suggests a correspondence with Moses' actions and words in Deuteronomy 9–10, but as "a parallel in proper leadership" (Nelson, *Joshua*, 102).

74. Mitchell rightly observes, I think, that Joshua's statement draws YHWH into "a legal case" as covenant partner—though his notion that YHWH thus "has to prove his innocence" seems improbable (Mitchell, *Together in the Land*, 68).

75. The phrasing of Achan's and Joshua's responses to the crime highlights this corporate character again—and perhaps Achan's failure to realize it. Achan's "*I* have sinned against YHWH" (*ʾānōkî ḥāṭāʾtî laYHWH*, 7:20), while an appropriate confession of his role as transgressor, does not fully recognize the corporate implications of his crime, as expressed in Joshua's words, "Why have you made trouble for *us*?" (*meh ʿăkartānû*, v. 25).

76. This "corporate character" is grounded in Israel's identity as the covenant community formed by YHWH's election, not based upon a primitive inability to distinguish the individual from the group—a notion that Achan's selection as guilty party in this story easily refutes. Kaminsky offers a helpful discussion of the matter of Israel's corporate character in Joshua 7 in *Corporate Responsibility in the Hebrew Bible*, 67–95. Among other points, Kaminsky emphasizes the necessity of Israel's holiness as a people to render it a fit environment for the dwelling of the divine presence—a state that is thrown into jeopardy by the presence of *ḥerem* objects (Kaminsky, *Corporate Responsibility*, 93–94).

77. Butler, *Joshua*, 89, and Nelson, *Joshua*, 103, both point out the broader implications of this story for action on the part of Israelite readers in rectifying Israel's contemporary infidelity to YHWH.

Chapter 3. The Gibeonites and the Transjordanian Altar

1. The book of Joshua contains a striking mix of divine speech and silence; sometimes YHWH is quite vocal and directive, while at other times He is silent either for His own reasons or because Israel fails to consult Him. While the book opens with YHWH's commissioning of Joshua, YHWH's words thereafter are sometimes spoken to Joshua (e.g., chaps. 3, 7, 13) and sometimes conveyed through him to Israel (e.g., chaps. 3, 24), but as in the stories discussed in this chapter, they are sometimes absent in any spoken form. As will be noted below, Dtr has placed the book of the Torah in Joshua's hand from square one, so that it can be assumed to be available for consultation throughout the story, even though it is rarely explicitly present.

2. Joshua Berman compares the *herem* of Achan to that of Ai (*Narrative Analogy*, 53), pointing out the distinctive language used to describe the raising of a "cairn" over Achan and over the king of Ai at the conclusion of each story (31–32). Spina instead draws an analogy between the *herem* of Achan and that of Jericho (*Faith of the Outsider*, 69). Both comparisons are apt, though Berman's is most persuasive as the more detailed study of similarities.

3. Notably, two of the five mentions of the "book of the Law" in Joshua occur in this section, in verses 31 and 34.

4. The steep drop-off from a sense of settledness or security to turmoil between these two chapters is akin to the break between chapters 6 and 7, the conquest of Jericho followed by defeat at Ai and revelation of Achan's sin (discussed above), and between chapters 21 and 22, the completion of the division of the land followed by the dispute over the Transjordanian altar (discussed below). These sudden shifts, sharply juxtaposing Israel's obedient and problematic actions, create an effect similar to that of the juxtaposition of Joshua 24:31 and these legally ambiguous stories: a portrait of Israel as both faithful *and* fallible.

5. Verse 14 tells us that "the Israelites heard," but as is common in reports of leaked information in the Hebrew Bible, it does not specify the source of the rumor or report.

6. Notably, this chapter immediately follows Israel's own pronouncement of the blessings and curses of the covenant upon itself at the ceremony of Joshua 8:30–35. Israel's difficult task of dealing with its own transgression here recalls the way in which it has taken upon its own lips the words of divine judgment and beneficence in the previous chapter. Hawk similarly notes correspondences between Joshua 9 and Deuteronomy 29 which "evoke the grid of obedience while telling the story of a serious transgression," but he apparently

overlooks the more immediate covenant connections in Joshua 8 (Hawk, *Every Promise*, 88).

7. Hawk considers the Israelites to be justified in grumbling at what he takes to be the disobedience of their leaders in this case, setting this episode in ironic contrast to the disobedient grumbling of the wilderness generation (Hawk, *Every Promise*, 86). His assessment of the episode, however, insufficiently explains the remarkable similarity between this complaint and its predecessors, and more significantly, fails to account for what appears to be YHWH's approval, through His fighting for Israel on Gibeon's behalf, of the solution chosen. Woudstra is more likely correct in taking this onset of grumbling as a sign of emerging discontent and rebelliousness among the people (Woudstra, *Joshua*, 168 and n38).

8. As Hawk seems to assume in his insistence that the text "represses the sense of Israel's disobedience once again" through the resolution that Joshua opts for (Hawk, *Every Promise*, 90–91).

9. One must wonder whether the absence from the text of a word from heaven regarding what should or should not have been done points to the moral ambiguity of treaty-making throughout Israelite traditions.

10. This suggestion that a sin could somehow be reversed by the untimely taking of an action whose time is now past echoes the attempt of the ancestors to enter the promised land after their initial refusal to do so in Numbers 14:39–45.

11. Polzin understands this triumph of "solemn promise" over "strict interpretation of the Mosaic covenant" in the case of the Gibeonites as analogous to (and perhaps grounded in?) Moses' invocation of the promise to the ancestors in Deuteronomy 9:27–28 to persuade YHWH to sustain His covenant mercifully with disobedient Israel (Polzin, *Moses and the Deuteronomist*, 119). Similarly, Polzin sees this dynamic at work in Deuteronomy 29, where in spite of Israel's inability to respond properly to YHWH's saving actions on its behalf (v. 4), YHWH nonetheless enters into covenant with Israel (v. 13) (119–20). See Polzin, *Moses and the Deuteronomist*, 117–23, for his full discussion of the connections between Deuteronomy 29 and Joshua 9, and for his quite illuminating reading of the ways in which the story presents Gibeon as a type of Israel.

The outcome of this story may also reflect the dynamic of faithfulness to a treaty taking precedence over the appropriateness of making a treaty with a foreign nation. Ezekiel 17:11–21 displays a similar hierarchy of concerns, wherein an Israelite ruler is condemned for violating a treaty made with a foreign country, even though in the previous chapter the prophet describes Israel's relations with other nations in harsh metaphors of harlotry (Ezek 16:23–29). As in the case of the treaty with Gibeon, it seems that the shifting of allegiances after a treaty has been made only compounds the violation of establishing alliances with foreign nations in the first place.

12. Mitchell notes the rescue of the Gibeonites in the following chapter (Josh 10) "primarily as an illustration of Israel's covenant loyalty," an analysis that would further extend the point made here.

13. See chapter 4 for further discussion of this, particularly the question of whether this state of coexistence is contrary to or compatible with YHWH's purposes for and promises to Israel.

14. Contrary to Mitchell, who describes the Gibeonites' confession of faith as "impeccable" (Mitchell, *Together in the Land*, 85) and compares it favorably to Rahab's (Mitchell, *Together in the Land*, 169). In contrasting the nations' "hearing" and "fearing" in Joshua with Israel's "seeing" and "knowing" in the book of Joshua, Mitchell correctly observes that Rahab "knows" (Josh 2:9) like Israel in addition to "hearing" and "fearing" with her compatriots (Mitchell, *Together in the Land*, 142–51). He fails to note, however, that the Gibeonites in fact speak only of "hearing" (9:9, where they in fact falsely report what they have heard; cf. 9:3), never of "knowing" or "seeing" YHWH's acts—a key feature that distinguishes their speech from Rahab's confession. Creach makes a similar comparison between Rahab's and the Gibeonites' positive response to "hearing" (Creach, *Joshua*, 37) but likewise does not observe the distinction in "knowing."

15. Consider the child Samuel as another example of a living votive offering (1 Sam 1:24–28), or Samson's lifelong dedication as a Nazirite while still in utero (Jdg 13:1–5); cf. also in the New Testament the "living sacrifice" of the Christian's life in Romans 12:1.

16. For a few examples from Jewish and Christian history, see Collins's "Zeal of Phinehas," 12–14.

17. See, for example, Taylor, *A Secular Age*, especially chapter 3, on what he describes as "the Great Disembedding"—in short, the extraction of the individual's practice of religion from the broader social and cosmic frameworks of which it had previously been an integral part.

18. Cf. Deuteronomy 32:8–9.

19. Younger, *Ancient Conquest Accounts*.

20. E.g., Merneptah's claim to have wiped out Israel as stated on the Merneptah Stele; see Younger, *Ancient Conquest Accounts*, 227–28, for a very concise and helpful sampling of comparative examples from various cultures.

21. Witness, for example, the effect of the Rab Shakeh's speech in 2 Kings 19:1–4, which drives Hezekiah and the Judean officials to don sackcloth and inspires the king to describe the situation in the dire terms of the birthing process gone wrong.

22. See Billings, "Review," 91–94.

23. For a more in-depth discussion of the language of ḥerem in its biblical usage and extrabiblical parallels, see Stern, *The Biblical Ḥerem*; for a briefer but still thorough treatment, see Lohfink, "Ḥaram," 5:180–99.

24. See especially Weinfeld, *Promise of the Land*, 88–93, who discusses the retrospective shift of the ḥerem in Deuteronomy from vow to unconditional institution. See also Lohfink, who notes the occasional nature of the early practice of ḥerem ("Ḥaram," 5:194); and Niditch, *War in the Hebrew Bible*, 31–34, for a discussion of links between war vows and the ban.

25. See Lohfink, "Ḥaram," 5:180–99, for a concise discussion of the use of the Hiphil of ḥrm in the Mesha Stele.

26. See Deuteronomy 7:1–6 for the basic Deuteronomic formulation of this injunction.

27. A significant majority of the occurrences of words derived from the root ḥrm in the Hebrew Bible are found in the books of the DtrH; thirty-three out of forty-eight uses of the Hiphil are found there, along with eighteen out of the twenty-nine uses of the noun ḥerem (Lohfink, "Ḥaram," 5:181).

28. The run-on prologue to the anti-Canaanite commands of Deuteronomy 7 in verses 1–2 offers a prime example of this. Here, the command to obliterate the Canaanites (v. 2) is juxtaposed with commands that presume their survival (vv. 3–5). In *Deuteronomy and the Meaning of "Monotheism,"* MacDonald offers an astute hermeneutical solution to the dilemma this poses, but one that does not sufficiently account for the origin of the juxtaposition; I discuss his proposed reading further below.

29. See Deuteronomy 2:34, 3:6, Joshua 2:10.

30. The contrast in Numbers 21 between the use of ḥerem terminology for the destruction of Arad but not in relation to Sihon and Og within a single chapter, makes the same point in the opposite way as well: it demonstrates that outside of DtrH, the ḥerem is not perceived as a practice to be universally applied during Israel's taking of the land.

31. Moberly, "Shema," 134; and MacDonald, *Monotheism*, 108–23.

32. Moberly, "Shema," 133–37.

33. MacDonald, *Monotheism*, 113–17.

34. Moberly, "Shema," 135. MacDonald's reading expands upon the basic framework established by Moberly's interpretation of the prohibition and command regarding treatment of the Canaanites in Deuteronomy 7:3–4.

35. Moberly, "Shema," 135.

36. Moberly, "Shema," 135–36; MacDonald, *Monotheism*, 117–22.

37. Moberly, "Shema," 136.

38. Moberly, "Shema," 136.

39. Moberly, "Shema," 135–36; MacDonald, *Monotheism*, 117–22. In addition, Douglas S. Earl presents an anthropological and literary "solution" to

the ḥerem problem in *Reading Joshua as Christian Scripture* which casts the outworking of the command in the text of Joshua in metaphorical terms of identity formation and differentiation rather than slaughter. Unfortunately, Earl does not interact with either Moberly's or MacDonald's work, and does not seem to recognize the internal tension already present in the ḥerem command as codified in Deuteronomy 7:1–5.

40. Moberly, "Shema," 136–37. MacDonald, *Monotheism*, 119–20. Both authors credibly exclude Josiah's killing of the priests at illicit shrines from his supposed implementation of the ḥerem, finding the rationale instead in the words of the man of God in 1 Kings 13:2 (Moberly, "Shema," 137; MacDonald, *Monotheism*, 120).

41. Moberly himself offers this interpretation provisionally and acknowledges that his proposal requires further investigation to substantiate it (Moberly, "Shema," 136n23). Even MacDonald's more detailed development of Moberly's thesis, which he undertakes in the course of his excellent study of Deuteronomy, mainly extends and expands upon Moberly's interpretation in relation to other texts without first looking to other texts to test the validity of Moberly's thesis.

42. See Moberly, "Shema," 136.

43. Within this passage, ḥerem terminology occurs once in verse 16, as a verbal form, and once in verse 18, as a noun.

44. Deuteronomy 7:1 lists seven nations: the Hittites, Girgashites, Amorites, Canaanites, Perizzites, Hivites, and Jebusites. In the list found in 20:16, the nations number six, lacking the Girgashites; apart from this, the naming and order of the nations are the same.

45. The comprehensiveness of the "incidental" ḥerem vow seems to vary in this respect; sometimes the taking of any plunder for personal use is forbidden (e.g., the destruction of Jericho in Josh 6:15–19, Saul's battle against the Amalekites in 1 Sam 15:3), while sometimes it is permitted (e.g., in the case of Og's and Sihon's cities in Deut 2:35 and 3:7, in the case of Ai in Josh 8:2).

46. Joshua 10:28, 35, 37, 39, 40; 11:11, 12, 20, 21–22. Significantly, the wording of the texts in these chapters seems to be tailored to match the wording of the stipulations in Deuteronomy 20:16–18.

47. Moberly, "Shema," 136–37. MacDonald, *Monotheism*, 119–20. A later date for the ḥerem does not, however, preclude Weinfeld's suggestion that the idea of the *expulsion* of the Canaanites originates in the eighth and seventh centuries BCE (Weinfeld, *Promise of the Land*, 93).

48. Richard Nelson, whose approach to DtrH builds upon and expands Cross's, indirectly resolves the challenge of relating Joshua to the DtrH by bringing the monarchy quite directly into the book of Joshua in his article "Josiah in the Book of Joshua." In Nelson's words, "The Joshua of Dtr is in many

ways a thinly disguised Josianic figure who acts out the events of Dtr's own day on the stage of the classical past" (Nelson, "Josiah," 536). The parallel Nelson draws between Joshua and Josiah, however, consists of little more than rough similarities when closely examined. For example, it is difficult to be impressed by Nelson's assertion that "Josh 5:10–12 corresponds exactly to Josiah's celebration" of the Passover, when the primary feature that the two share is simply that DtrH recounts their Passover observances at all.

Nelson's arguments are adopted and developed at greater length by Lori Rowlett, *Rhetoric of Violence*, in a fruitful work that nonetheless suffers from its dependence on some of Nelson's supposed parallels.

49. Yair Hoffman opts for a later date for the *ḥerem* material, but partly because he dates the entire book of Joshua to the post-exilic period—a move that I find creative, but not credible ("Deuteronomistic Concept," 196–210).

50. In addition to the examples already listed in note 254, see von Rad, *Deuteronomy*, 25, who connects the "warlike spirit of Deuteronomy" with Josiah's rule; and Weinfeld, *Deuteronomy and the Deuteronomic School*, 50–51, who links various sections of Joshua—including chapters 10–12, which make frequent use of *ḥerem* language that mirrors the Deuteronomic injunctions—with Assyrian rhetoric of the eighth to seventh centuries, pointing presumably to a pre-exilic stratum of DtrH. Nelson, while only explicitly developing the link between Deuteronomy 7 and Josianic policy on the subject of intermarriage (Deut 7:3) (Nelson, "Josiah," 539–40), also points to similarities between Joshua's and Josiah's military-religious role (Nelson, "Josiah," 537–38) and use of violence to purify the cult (Nelson, "Josiah," 539–40).

51. Besides this phrase, Joshua 10–11 expresses the totality of the destruction in fulfillment of the *ḥerem* commands of Deuteronomy with two key phrases: *kol-hannepeš ʾăšer bāh* (Josh 10:28, 30, 32, 35, 37, 39; 11:11), and *lōʾ hišʾîr śārîd* (Josh 10:28, 30, 33, 37, 39, 40; 11:8). These occur in subsidiary statements about the destruction of individual sites leading up to summary statements employing the Deuteronomy 20:16 phrase *kol-nĕšāmâ* in Joshua 10:40, 11:11, and 11:14. The distribution of these various phrases in Joshua 10–11 seems better explained as a conscious literary pattern than as the use of different terminology by multiple redactors.

52. Within DtrH, the word *nĕšāmâ* occurs only three times (2 Sam 22:16, 1 Kgs 15:29, 1 Kgs 17:17) outside of these four passages. Interestingly, one of these other contexts employs the precise phrase *kol-nĕšāmâ*: Jehu's obliteration of the house of Jeroboam in 1 Kings 15:39.

53. Levenson, "Book of the Torah," 203n1; his article builds particularly upon insights from Hans Walter Wolff in "Das Kerygma des deuteronomistischen Geschichtswerks," *ZAW* 73 (1961): 171–86; and Norbert Lohfink, "Auslegung deuteronomischer Texte, IV," *BibLeb* 4 (1964): 247–56; as well as Frank Moore Cross, *CMHE*.

54. Levenson, "Who Inserted the Book of the Torah?," 232.

55. Although John Goldingay refrains from assigning a date to the literary creation of the ḥerem texts in Deuteronomy, he matter-of-factly states, "We can be sure enough that they come from a period when their audience had no prospects of actually annihilating the Canaanites" (Goldingay, "Justice and Salvation for Israel and Canaan," 177–78). MacDonald provides further rationale for such an interpretation when he points out that the stereotypical and ideological nature of the lists of Canaanite nations which occur throughout the Hebrew Bible supports a metaphorical interpretation of these "nations" (MacDonald, *Monotheism*, 112).

56. Collins makes a similar mistake in the account of the ḥerem commands he gives in "Zeal of Phinehas." There he reads the phrasing of Deuteronomy 20 as "rationalizing" the ban by limiting its application to only "near neighbors" as a precautionary measure against the risk of cultic contamination (Collins, "Zeal of Phinehas," 7). It seems to me, though, that this passage does not involve a mitigation of ḥerem language, as Collins suggests, but rather forms part of a pattern of the *intensification* and theological redefinition of such language by Dtr. Rather than "rationalizing" earlier mentions of the ban, I see Dtr as intentionally implementing ḥerem language as part of a literary-theological strategy even where it was not present in his source texts.

57. A "fresh reconfiguration and reappropriation" of the language of ḥerem, as Moberly aptly describes it (Moberly, "Shema," 136).

58. Cross, *Canaanite Myth*, 105–11, 169–77.

59. Levenson, *Death and Resurrection*, 43–52.

60. For example, Collins, "Zeal of Phinehas," 10–11, citing James Barr as well (Barr, *Biblical Faith and Natural Theology*, 214), judges the *texts themselves* to be problematic in their portrayal of Israel's actions and YHWH's commands, regardless of the historical underpinnings behind this portrayal or the interpretive strategies that might unfold in the face of it.

61. Goldingay, for example, notes the significant difference that Israel's political power or lack thereof makes in the tone of the Deuteronomic ḥerem texts ("Justice and Salvation for Israel and Canaan," 177–78).

62. Both MacDonald, *Monotheism*, 112, and Stern, *Biblical Ḥerem*, 103, propose a metaphorical-mythic understanding of these lists of primordial nations. Stern, *Biblical Ḥerem*, 217, suggests on the basis of this understanding that the limitation of the ḥerem to these particular nations serves, in fact, to curtail its practice in any literal form.

63. For example, Lemche, *Canaanites and Their Land*, 119–20, takes the stories of Israel's "ideological struggle" with the Canaanites as "exemplary narratives" showing readers how to deal with "persons of non-Israelite origin." Such an interpretation, in my opinion, does the text a disservice in dealing

with it as a "blunt object" rather than seeing it as the sophisticated theological and literary construction that it is.

64. See Deuteronomy 20:15-18.

65. This parallel between internal and external idolaters enables the connection that Rowlett draws between the rhetoric of violence employed in the war chapters of Joshua and the policies of Josiah (Rowlett, *Rhetoric of Violence*, esp. 171-80). She reads the Joshua narrative as a polemic against aberrant "insiders" crafted to support the Josianic regime (Rowlett, *Rhetoric of Violence*, 183).

66. Expressing this view toward rather different ends are Younger, *Ancient Conquest Accounts*, 253-57, who takes it as a challenge to "peasant revolt" models of Israel's origins, and Collins, "Zeal of Phinehas," 7-8, who understands Israel's use of the ḥerem as a means of "the advancement of a particular people and the imposition of its cult within the territory it controls" (Collins, "Zeal of Phinehas," 8).

67. Deuteronomy indeed speaks of the "wickedness" of the Canaanites, but only in a comparison indicating Israel's lack of intrinsic merit in relation to them (9:5). What the precise nature of this "wickedness" may be and how it relates to the Canaanites' displacement is not made clear, despite MacDonald's attempts to argue against the Canaanites' displacement as an act of YHWH's judgment upon them (MacDonald, *Monotheism*, 116-17). As Goldingay correctly observes, the text enumerates various factors involved or not involved in why Israel comes into possession of the land, but "in what way [Israel's possession] relates to the nations' rěšaʿ is unstated" ("Justice and Salvation for Israel and Canaan," 177).

68. See Deuteronomy 7:7-11, 17-19; 8:17-18; and 9:4-6, which all present Israel's weakness and inadequacy against the strength of YHWH's promises and actions.

69. In contrast, Hawk finds YHWH's "complicity in the decision to save Gibeon" to be "surprising," further adding to Israel's sense of false security as it continues to transgress the ḥerem commands (Hawk, *Every Promise*, 90-91). He fails to recognize, though, Israel's repentant restraint in its treatment of the Gibeonites, stemming its anger to honor its oath before YHWH. Further, his assessment of the situation seems unlikely in light of YHWH's demonstrated willingness to punish Israel swiftly and severely through military defeat in the case of Achan (cf. Josh 7); a similar outcome would presumably have ensued here, had YHWH disapproved of Israel's decision regarding the treatment of the Gibeonites.

70. Significant indications of incompleteness can be found in the following texts: prior to the division of the land, in 13:1-5; reiterated in the chapter following the altar dispute, in 23:4-5, 9-11; and expressed by the ongoing

presence of non-Israelites in the land as indicated by 23:7, 12–13, as well as at several points in the allotment lists (e.g., 15:63; 16:10; 17:12–13, 16).

71. See Hawk, *Every Promise*, 114–15, who avers that in light of the preceding picture of disobedience and partial occupation in the book of Joshua, this "concluding summary is astonishing" (114). Likewise, Polzin, *Moses and the Deuteronomist*, 126–28, and 132–33, states this perspective even more strongly when he describes 21:43—and statements like it that affirm the complete fulfillment of YHWH's promises—as a "sweeping and grossly unrealistic assertion" (127). He reads it as a prime locus for the clash of the two "voices" he perceives in the text; by placing this summary after the piecemeal occupation of the land in Joshua 13–21, the "voice of critical traditionalism" ridicules the claims of the "voice of authoritarian dogmatism" to the extent that Polzin declares that "the Book of Joshua is scarcely intelligible if 21:41–43 is not read in an ironic sense" (Polzin, *Moses and the Deuteronomist*, 132).

72. The next chapter of the present work further explores the subject of how the book of Joshua portrays the extent of Israel's conquest of the land.

73. For example, note Israel's initial assumption that divine abandonment and not human transgression has brought about the defeat at Ai (Josh 7:6–9), as well as Israel's hasty sealing of an alliance with the Gibeonites without consulting YHWH (Josh 9:14–15).

74. Interestingly, the disputed altar at the center of the story is one of only two altars that are mentioned in the entire book of Joshua, both of them Israelite; the other is built by Joshua at Mount Ebal in chapter 8. Contrary to what we might expect from Deuteronomy 12, no destruction of Canaanite cult sites takes place at any point in the book. This absence of Canaanite cultic installations from the book of Joshua lends support to my conclusions about the inner-Israelite message of the *ḥerem* put forth above.

75. Nelson, *Joshua*, 249–50, likewise concludes that the story is told from a "thoroughly west-of-Jordan" vantage point. Boling and Wright, *Joshua*, 512, also observe the sudden restriction of "the Bene Israel" to the Cisjordanian tribes alone in verse 11. On the other hand, Hawk, *Joshua*, 238, correctly observes that a "kaleidoscope of shifting perspectives swirls" through the story, mirroring the jumble of questions the story raises about geography, Israelite identity, and the meaning of the altar.

76. Various commentators describe "unity" as the central theme or point of the story, though with different emphases. Elie Assis explicates "the unity of the people despite geographical separation" as the narrative's "main idea," while recognizing the irony that the concern for unity becomes a source of division in this story (Assis, "'For It Shall Be a Witness,'" 231). Woudstra similarly concludes that the focus of the story is unity and the possibility of it being undermined by illicit cult places (Woudstra, *Joshua*, 319). Nelson also understands the story as promoting "an awareness of and commitment to national

unity in the face of opposing attitudes and circumstances" (Nelson, *Joshua*, 249). While this theme is indeed central to the story, I think the point of the story lies beyond the idea of unity per se. Butler hints at this fuller meaning when he says that the altar serves as a witness not only of *national* unity but that "the unifying factor is YHWH" (Butler, *Joshua*, 249).

77. See, for example, Gray, *Joshua*, 51; Nelson, *Joshua*, 164; Noth, *Deuteronomistic History*, 40; and Soggin, *Joshua*, 151. For an alternative view, see Butler, *Joshua*, 147, who understands the bracketing formulae in 13:1 and 23:1b as serving to unite Joshua's final action of dividing the land to his parting words.

78. See Assis, "Position and Function of Jos 22," 529–31, for a brief discussion and extensive bibliography dealing with the various possible configurations of how the Dtr and P features of the text relate to the text's history of development. See also Campbell and O'Brien, *Unfolding the Deuteronomistic History*, 156–57, for identification of language in the story that elsewhere is predominantly or exclusively priestly. On this basis, they conclude that "the core of 22:9–34 could be old tradition; the present formulation is late" (Campbell and O'Brien, *Unfolding the Deuteronomistic History*, 157).

79. See, for example, Gray, *Joshua*, 51–52; Nelson, *Joshua*, 247. Kloppenborg, "Joshua 22," attributes the shape of the story almost exclusively to P. In contrast, Soggin finds a lighter influence of P, "concerned simply with making sure that the priest plays the role which is his due," while Dtr makes significant contributions to the present form of the story (Soggin, *Joshua*, 214–15).

80. Campbell and O'Brien, *Unfolding the Deuteronomistic History*, 157.

81. Assis, "Position and Function of Jos 22," 539–40, also finds numerous resonances between the two stories, though perhaps more than can be convincingly substantiated.

82. Scholars have offered a variety of possible explanations of the story's earliest purpose, occasion, and/or etiological function; any of a number of these might fit with the theory proposed here, since the story's function in Joshua depends more on Dtr's use of it than on its context of origin.

83. Butler, *Joshua*, 243–44, takes the story as directly addressing the problem of worship in exile. Similarly, Nelson interprets the story within a diaspora setting as showing that "Jews outside the land have a 'share in YHWH'" (Nelson, *Joshua*, 250).

84. Assis, "Position and Function of Jos 22," 531–34, outlines several points of connection with themes manifested elsewhere of the book. Note that this view does not preclude the possibility that a P redactor added a later, light overlay when joining DtrH with the priestly Torah.

85. Assis, "Position and Function of Jos 22," undertakes the same task in his article, but with a different focus and conclusions.

86. For example, Nelson notes that "key pieces to the puzzle" are withheld from the reader until verses 27-28 (Nelson, *Joshua*, 253).

87. Alter discusses reticence specifically with reference to characterization in *The Art of Biblical Narrative* (Alter, *Art*, 114-30), but some of his observations are more broadly applicable.

88. Nelson observes the significance of the loyalty of the Transjordanians here as background to their ensuing construction of the altar, but does not explore it further (Nelson, *Joshua*, 247).

89. See the reference to YHWH giving "rest" to Israel as part of the fulfillment of His promises to the ancestors only a few verses earlier in 21:44.

90. Nelson sees this perspective as advocated so repeatedly in this text that he takes it to characterize the views not only of the Cisjordanian tribes depicted within the story but of the narrator himself (Nelson, *Joshua*, 249). Others perceive it as an element that is primitive (Butler, *Joshua*, 245; Soggin, *Joshua*, 212-13) or quite late (Gray, *Joshua*, 170-71; also Nelson, *Joshua*, 250). Hawk offers a literary alternative to these historical analyses, suggesting that the tension between the western tribes' demarcation of the Jordan as the far boundary of "YHWH's land" and YHWH's own command, recalled in 22:9, indicates that "the tribal group in the west, *and not YHWH*, has made the Jordan a boundary between the tribes" (Hawk, *Joshua*, 242).

91. Disagreement persists about which side of the river, east or west, the altar is located on. For example, Gray, *Joshua*, 171, locates the altar west of the Jordan because of the postexilic setting, with Israel confined to Cisjordan, which he posits for the story; Snaith likewise situates it on the western bank (Snaith, "Altar at Gilgal," 331). Woudstra, *Joshua*, 321, on the other hand, opts mildly for the eastern bank. Both Nelson, *Joshua*, 251-52, and Hawk, *Joshua*, 237, conclude that information about the altar's location is abundant but indecipherable.

92. Renderings of this phrase have exhibited greater and lesser degrees of helpfulness—and gracefulness: "imposing" (NIV), "of great size" (NRSV), "of conspicuous appearance" (Woudstra, *Joshua*, 321), "conspicuously large" or roughly "big-looking" (Hawk, *Joshua*, 236 and n13), "huge-looking" (Nelson, *Joshua*, 251).

93. Barbara Organ also notes the lack of "recourse to YHWH's oracle" here (Organ, "Pursuing Phinehas," 214).

94. Note also his military involvement in the follow-up to this incident in Numbers 31, where the Midianites are requited for their role at Peor (Num 31:1-2, 15-16).

95. Organ, "Pursuing Phinehas," 209. Her reading follows the figure of Phinehas through the various biblical texts in which he appears. Interestingly, she finds his role in Joshua 22 somewhat different from the other contexts,

which all involve women and war. I will explore some of the reasons for Phinehas's appearance in this particular text below.

96. Since this story lies outside the bounds of DtrH, most likely this reference should be attributed to the priestly form of the story prior to Dtr, in accord with Phinehas's role here. No strong verbal ties exist between the two stories, which seem to be linked largely by the cultic nature of the offense and by the presence of Phinehas. Each concludes with the image of the Lord's anger being halted by the resolution of their respective situations, but Numbers 25:11 uses *ḥămāt* and *qānʾeh* to designate the divine response averted, while Joshua 22:31 speaks in terms of "rescue . . . from the hand of YHWH."

97. Organ, "Pursuing Phinehas," 214, appears to treat him as the speaker for the western delegation in this episode, contrasting his role as a "man of words" in this text with his former portrait in Numbers 25 and 31 as a "man of action." While this contrast is accurate to some extent, no speech in Joshua 22 is actually attributed to Phinehas alone until verse 31, after the debate has run its course.

98. Contrary to Hawk's assessment that "good in the eyes of" signals only an "attitude" and not necessarily persuasion (Hawk, *Joshua*, 244). There appear to be two errors in his list of five comparative usages. Of the correct references, parallel usages of this expression seem to show that it carries with it the sense of decision in the case of a disputed point, not of merely adequate satisfaction versus full conviction.

99. The rhetoric of the western tribes overall excludes the eastern tribes from Israel and from YHWH's people, titles that they co-opt for those who dwell west of the Jordan locating Israel's identity in the land west of the Jordan rather than in YHWH (as Hawk perceptively observes, *Joshua*, 239–40). This analogy of the altar-building with past sins committed in united Israel seems to draw the closest connection between the two groups, with its assumption that the eastern tribes are able to affect the "community of Israel" (22:18), including the Cisjordanian tribes, by their actions.

100. Hawk, *Joshua*, 241–42.

101. The only other use of *tabnît* in relation to an altar is in the account of Ahaz's copying of the Damascene altar in 2 Kings 16:10–16. While this act could cast ominous overtones on this story within the context of DtrH, the copying of YHWH's own altar should be distinguished from the imitation of a foreign altar and its subsequent substitution for YHWH's altar in the Temple.

102. See Psalms 144:12 and Ezekiel 8:3, 10:8.

103. Additional positive or neutral uses include David's plans for the temple in 1 Chronicles 28:11–12, 19; comparisons of one thing to another in Ezekiel 8:3, 10:8; and Psalms 144:12. With reference to idolatrous "images," the

term also occurs in Psalms 106:20 and Isaiah 44:13, and it is used of Ahaz's copied foreign altar in 2 Kings 16:10.

104. Nelson sees the text as presenting the argument as genuinely persuasive (Nelson, *Joshua*, 253); Hawk finds it to be presented as acceptable but not necessarily convincing (Hawk, *Joshua*, 244).

105. Note that this stone structure is referred to as a *zikkārôn*, a "monument" or "memorial" in 4:7, while the altar is spoken of as an *ʿēd*, or "witness," in 22:27–28. It is possible that this difference in terminology is dependent upon the altar's name, if *ʿēd* was indeed part of it. The question of the altar's name, though, is complicated; commentators disagree about whether the structure of the text indicates that the full sentence of verse 34 is the name of the altar (e.g., Woudstra, *Joshua*, 330), or whether the name has been lost from the text (e.g., Nelson, *Joshua*, 248; Soggin, *Joshua*, 212). In any case, it seems to me that other features shared by both stories (an interest in unified Israel, a concern for future generations, and a stone structure near the Jordan) naturally elicit a comparison between the texts.

Chapter 4. The Extent of Israel's Occupation of the Land

1. See Polzin, *Moses and the Deuteronomist*, 126–34.
2. Polzin, *Moses and the Deuteronomist*, 131–32.
3. Polzin, *Moses and the Deuteronomist*, 126, 128.
4. Polzin, *Moses and the Deuteronomist*, 132.
5. Polzin, *Moses and the Deuteronomist*, 132.
6. Outside of the book of Joshua, several other explanations are given that attribute the lack of completeness to YHWH, framing it not as His failure to give what he promised, but rather as an act of *mercy* or *provision* on YHWH's part. For example, YHWH wishes to prevent wild animals from overrunning the empty land (Exod 23:29, Deut 7:22), or to equip future generations of Israelites with training for war (Jdg 3:2), or to continue to test Israel's faithfulness (Jdg 2:22, 3:4).
7. A possibility perhaps threatened by Joshua's exhortation in Joshua 18:1–7, in which he urges the remaining tribes to act swiftly to receive their part of the promised land. In that context, the potential for disobedience is defused by the quick and obedient response of the tribes addressed. It uncomfortably prods readers, though, to begin to wonder what will happen after Joshua is gone.
8. The conclusion that these scattered notices anticipate Israel's failure to obey, even if they do not yet assert it, is supported by their similarity to the

larger block in Judges 1:17–36, which prefaces Israel's reprimand at Bochim (Jdg 2:1–5) and the account of Israel's failings after Joshua's passing which introduces the cycles of judges (2:10–19).

9. As Walter Brueggemann puts it, "Land is in history with YHWH. It is never contextless space" (Brueggemann, *The Land*, 55). One wishes that Brueggemann had explored this apt observation more thoroughly in relation to the book of Joshua, which his discussion of the land largely—and regrettably—neglects.

10. See Joshua 23:12–13, 16, and 24:19–20, for the threatened consequences of Israel's choice of other gods.

11. Reflected, for example, in the "covenant prologue" recounting YHWH's past actions for Israel in Joshua 24:2–13.

12. Often the first twelve chapters of Joshua continue to be described as recounting the "conquest of the promised land" (e.g., Mitchell, *Together in the Land*, 96, speaks of "the narrative of conquest"), even as critical scholarship challenges this description of both the manner of Israel's occupation of the land and the biblical accounts that recall it. In fact, as we have seen in our study of the dynamics of obedience in these narratives, both the content and purpose of these chapters are rather more complex than either a "common" or "critical" description conveys. While it is true that, in contrast to the latter portion of the book, the military taking of the land indeed supplies the narrative framework for these early chapters, in many ways they deal far more substantially with themes of Israel's obedience and identity in relation to YHWH than with military exploits. Thus, we may plausibly expect that the themes of the first "section" of the book will continue into the latter portion as well, in spite of the different types of material employed.

13. Butler notes an emphasis on the aspect of curse rather than blessing in this text, which he finds consonant with an exilic audience "who have experienced both blessing and curse" (Butler, *Joshua*, 253–54). Soggin likewise judges this text to have an exilic address, based on oblique references to the exile in verses 13–16—a point that could be challenged as proof of exilic origins (Soggin, *Joshua*, 218–19). He also perceptively observes, however, the way in which the text establishes an analogy between the choices and challenges facing the generation of the conquest and the generation of returning exiles as both prepare to enter the land (Soggin, *Joshua*, 219).

14. Hawk, *Every Promise*, see esp. 98–100.

15. Hawk, *Every Promise*, 99–100.

16. Hawk, *Every Promise*, 99.

17. Mitchell, *Together in the Land*, 106.

18. Mitchell, *Together in the Land*, 109.

19. Butler, *Joshua*, 131.
20. Butler, *Joshua*, 131.
21. Butler, *Joshua*, 146.
22. Hawk, on the other hand, perceives this portion as setting up an unflattering comparison between the successful conquests of Moses in Transjordan and Joshua's unfinished work in Cisjordan (Hawk, *Every Promise*, 99, 102).
23. Nelson makes a similar point when he says, "Taking the certainty of promise as a given . . . Joshua's present task in v. 6b is simply to cast the lots . . . The problem of the land that remains and YHWH's promise will take care of itself" (Nelson, *Joshua*, 167). In sum, "the current responsibility of Israel's leader is merely to obey" (Nelson, *Joshua*, 167). I would emend this only by emphasizing YHWH's active agency in bringing His promise to fruition, since YHWH's intervention at the start of chapter 13 suggests that YHWH's promise does not run on autopilot.
24. Nelson too recognizes the transition in roles Joshua undergoes in this passage, regarding this text as a pivot point marking the completion of one divinely given task and the initiation of another (Nelson, *Joshua*, 156).
25. Even though his discussion of this text focuses on Joshua's obedient performance of his role, Butler also recognizes the key part YHWH's leadership plays here (Butler, *Joshua*, 147, 152–53).
26. See Benin's *The Footprints of God: Divine Accommodation in Jewish and Christian Thought* for a historical survey of Jewish and Christian understandings of divine accommodation.
27. Significantly, Joshua's reproach of the remaining tribes on their slowness to claim their land at the beginning of chapter 18 is the only situation in the latter part of the book in which a deficiency in Israel's occupation of the land is immediately remedied.
28. These are found in Joshua 15:63, 16:10, and 17:12–13 (and its related narrative in 17:14–18), all of which bear a strong resemblance to the block of similar statements found at the end of Judges 1 (vv. 21–36).
29. These indications of broader Canaanite presence are found in 13:1–7, examined above, and 23:4–5, 7, 12–13.
30. My view contrasts with that of Yohanan Aharoni, who assumes generally friendly relations between the Israelite-occupied territories and these towns, describing the former as "enjoying some reciprocal relationship" with the latter (Aharoni, *Land of the Bible*, 233).
31. Scholars also commonly see a further subdivision in this material between 17:14–15 and verses 16–18, though its process of composition remains somewhat unclear (Gray, *Joshua*, 143–44; Nelson, *Joshua*, 203–5; Soggin, *Joshua*, 182–83).

32. Note that the parallel in Judges has the Benjaminites rather than the Judahites failing to oust the Canaanites from Jerusalem and continuing to dwell alongside them (Jdg 1:21).

33. Various interpretations of this phrase have been proposed; most recently, see Geoghehan's summary of the history of scholarship on the issue, laudably including earlier interpreters as well as modern scholarship, along with his own conclusions regarding the implications of this phrase for our understanding of DtrH in *The Time, Place, and Purpose of the Deuteronomistic History*.

34. Commentators offer a wide variety of interpretations of the purpose of these statements. Woudstra appropriately concludes that these texts "set the stage for the developments contained in the book of Judges" (Woudstra, *Joshua*, 266; also 254–55, 266–67), notifying the reader of the latent threat of the remaining Canaanite pockets. Butler offers the interesting proposal that these notices have been recontextualized from Judges 1 in order to offer a forward-looking "theological interpretation" (Butler, *Joshua*, 186)—sometimes positive and sometimes negative—of the sections in Joshua 15–17 to which they have been attached (Butler, *Joshua*, 186–87). Oddly, Gray opines that the subjection of the Canaanites to corvée labor in Joshua 16:10 (in contrast with Jdg 1:29) is a Dtr "adjustment" meant to provide a "satisfactory explanation" for the ongoing Canaanite presence among Israel (Gray, *Joshua*, 147; cf. Butler, above). This seems a rather unsatisfactory explanation of the difference, if both Joshua and Judges are regarded as part of Dtr's overall work.

35. Nelson too concludes that "Joshua's vision of the future in v. 18 moves beyond mere political domination to eventual total victory" (Nelson, *Joshua*, 205). Butler notes the connection between this entry point into disobedience in the failure to drive out the Canaanites fully in the book of Joshua and its culmination "in the withdrawal of the divine promise" in Judges 2:21–23 (Butler, *Joshua*, 191–92).

36. See Assis, "'How Long Are You Slack,'" 1–25, for a literary analysis of how these stories of initiative provide positive counterexamples to the indications of hesitation.

37. Butler also seems to recognize this occasion as an opportunity for obedience (Butler, *Joshua*, 204–5), though some commentators are too occupied with the source identity of the material and the location of its sanctuary to attend to its theological dimension (e.g., Gray, *Joshua*, 151–52; Soggin, *Joshua*, 189–90).

38. The consequences of disobedience and slackness come into even sharper relief in Joshua 23:1–13, where Joshua exhorts Israel to obedience by recalling YHWH's work in Canaan on Israel's behalf thus far and threatening the consequences of disobedience.

39. See Levenson, *Creation and the Persistence of Evil*, chapter 11, "The Dialectic of Covenantal Theonomy," for an insightful and more detailed exposition of the relationship between Israel's autonomy and heteronomy within the context of covenant.

40. See von Rad's essay "There Remains Still a Rest," 94–102.

41. Butler, *Joshua*, 234–36; Gray, *Joshua*, 168; and Soggin, *Joshua*, 206, all aptly recognize the origin of these verses in Dtr redaction. Butler's view most closely resembles my own in realizing the function of these verses as a theological summation of the preceding material (Butler, *Joshua*, 234, 236). His claim that "the entire book is to be read in light of these three verses" (Butler, *Joshua*, 236), however, gives them more interpretive weight than I am persuaded that they can bear.

42. That YHWH's word did not fail is a motif repeated elsewhere in DtrH as well (Josh 23:14, 1 Kgs 8:56, 2 Kgs 10:10), as noted by von Rad in "The Deuteronomistic Theology of History," 78n1.

43. Butler rightly notes as well that YHWH's faithful actions are the chief subject of these verses (Butler, *Joshua*, 235), as does Woudstra (Woudstra, *Joshua*, 314). Butler's statement, though, that the Dtr redactor "ignores" the evidence of incomplete occupation (almost identically described by Gray, *Joshua*, 168) in making these sweeping statements seems deficient. Woudstra presents a more balanced view in his discussion of this passage, acknowledging the paradoxical view of the occupation of the land in Joshua "as both complete and incomplete" (Woudstra, *Joshua*, 314).

44. As discussed at the beginning of this chapter, "The Extent of Israel's Occupation of the Land"; Polzin, *Moses and the Deuteronomist*, 132. (Cf. Soggin, on the other hand, who is content to label this passage as "Deuteronomic," with little further comment [Soggin, *Joshua*, 206]).

45. Polzin, *Moses and the Deuteronomist*, 128, 132.

46. Woudstra again recognizes the emphasis on YHWH's action and gifts in this text (Woudstra, *Joshua*, 349); Butler, *Joshua*, 272, and Soggin, *Joshua*, 235, take a similar view.

47. This section, the "historical prologue" or "antecedent history," constitutes the second element of the six-part suzerain-vassal treaty; see, for example, Levenson's outline of the parts of this type of treaty in *Sinai and Zion*, 26–30.

48. A number of commentators observe the paradoxical meeting of the themes of complete and unfinished conquest in chapter 23, though their analysis of this juxtaposition varies widely. Gray, for example, names it as "the paradox between faith and history" that Dtr makes various attempts to resolve here and elsewhere in DtrH (Gray, *Joshua*, 174). Soggin essentially suggests that Dtr rationalizes—or rather, theologizes—this tension, explaining it away

by YHWH's judgment of Israel through the remnants of the conquered nations (Soggin, *Joshua*, 218). Woudstra, on the other hand, simply concludes that the juxtaposition shows that "these are two compatible ways of viewing the same events" (!) (Woudstra, *Joshua*, 332–33).

49. This first parting speech of Joshua is widely recognized as a thoroughly Dtr contribution to the book, which has its place among the collection of key speeches that form the hermeneutical structure of DtrH. See, for example, Butler, *Joshua*, 253–54; Gray, *Joshua*, 173; Soggin, *Joshua*, 217–19.

50. We might describe this as the literary equivalent of the sort of etymological fallacies so famously described by James Barr in *The Semantics of Biblical Language*.

51. Sternberg, *Poetics of Biblical Narrative*, 50–52.

52. See Bird, "YRŠ and the Deuteronomic Theology of the Conquest" on the usage of *yrš* within the Dtr corpus.

53. Hawk presents an illuminating look at the way in which the conquest of kings fits into the message of the book of Joshua in "Conquest Reconfigured," 145–60.

Bibliography

Abegg, Martin G., Peter Flint, and Eugene Ulrich. *The Dead Sea Scrolls Bible: The Oldest Known Bible Translated for the First Time into English.* San Francisco: HarperOne, 2002.
Aharoni, Yohanan. *The Land of the Bible: A Historical Geography.* Edited and translated by A. F. Rainey. Rev. and enl. ed. Philadelphia: Westminster Press, 1979.
———. "The Province-List of Judah." *Vetus Testamentum* 9 (1959): 225–46.
Albright, William Foxwell. "The Israelite Conquest in Light of Archaeology." *Bulletin of the American Schools of Oriental Research* 74 (1939): 11–22.
Alt, Albrecht. "The Settlement of the Israelites in Palestine." In *Essays on Old Testament History and Religion,* translated by R. A. Wilson, 173–221. Garden City, N.Y.: Anchor Books, 1968.
Alter, Robert. *The Art of Biblical Narrative.* New York: Basic Books, 1981.
Alter, Robert, and Frank Kermode, eds. *The Literary Guide to the Bible.* Cambridge, Mass.: Belknap Press, 1990.
Assis, Elie. "'For It Shall Be a Witness between Us': A Literary Reading of Josh 22." *Scandinavian Journal of the Old Testament* 18, no. 2 (2004): 208–31.
———. "'How Long Are You Slack to Go to Possess the Land' (Jos. xviii 3): Ideal and Reality in the Distribution Descriptions in Joshua xiii–xix." *Vetus Testamentum* 53 (2003): 1–25.
———. "The Position and Function of Jos 22 in the Book of Joshua." *Zeitschrift für die alttestamentliche Wissenschaft* 116 (2004): 528–41.
Bakhtin, Mikhail M. *Problems of Dostoyevsky's Poetics.* Edited and translated by Caryl Emerson. Minneapolis: University of Minnesota Press, 1984.

BIBLIOGRAPHY

Barr, James. *Biblical Faith and Natural Theology: The Gifford Lectures for 1991: Delivered in the University of Edinburgh.* Oxford: Oxford University Press, 1994.

———. *The Semantics of Biblical Language.* London: Oxford, 1961.

Beek, Martinus Adrianus. "Rahab in the Light of Jewish Exegesis." In *Von Kanaan bis Kerala: Festschrift für Prof. Mag. Dr. J. P. M. van der Ploeg O.P.*, edited by W. C. Delsman et al., 37–44. Kevelaer: Butzon and Bercker, 1982.

Benin, Stephen D. *The Footprints of God: Divine Accommodation in Jewish and Christian Thought.* SUNY Series in Judaica: Hermeneutics, Mysticism, and Religion. Albany: State University of New York Press, 1993.

Berenbaum, Michael, and Frank Skolnik, eds. *Encyclopaedia Judaica.* 2nd ed. 22 vols. Detroit: Macmillan Reference USA, 2007.

Berman, Joshua. *Narrative Analogy in the Hebrew Bible: Battle Stories and Their Equivalent Non-Battle Narratives.* Leiden: Brill, 2004.

Billings, Rachel. "Josiah's Incomparable Passover." Paper presented at the annual national meeting of the SBL, San Antonio, Tex., November 2003.

———. "Review of *Does the Bible Justify Violence?*, by John J. Collins." *Christian Scholars Review* 36, no. 1 (Autumn 2006): 91–94.

Bird, Phyllis. "*YRŠ* and the Deuteronomic Theology of the Conquest." ThD diss., Harvard University, 1972.

Bloch-Smith, Elizabeth. "Israelite Ethnicity in Iron I: Archaeology Preserves What Is Remembered and What Is Forgotten in Israel's History." *Journal of Biblical Literature* 122 (2003): 401–25.

Boling, Robert G. "Joshua." *The Anchor Bible Dictionary on CD-ROM.* 1994. Print ed.: David Noel Freedman, ed. *Anchor Bible Dictionary.* 6 vols. New York: Doubleday, 1992.

Boling, Robert G., and G. Ernest Wright. *Joshua.* Anchor Bible 6. Garden City, N.Y.: Doubleday, 1982.

Bronner, Leila Leah. *From Eve to Esther: Rabbinic Reconstructions of Biblical Women.* Gender and the Biblical Tradition. Louisville, Ky.: Westminster John Knox Press, 1994.

Brooks, Peter. "The Idea of a Psychoanalytic Literary Criticism." In *Discourse in Psychoanalysis and Literature,* edited by Shlomith Rimmon-Kenan, 1–18. London: Methuen, 1987.

———. *Reading for the Plot: Design and Intention in Narrative.* New York: Random House, 1984.

Brueggemann, Walter. *Divine Presence amid Violence: Contextualizing the Book of Joshua.* Eugene, Ore.: Cascade Books, 2009.

———. *The Land: Place as Gift, Promise, and Challenge in Biblical Faith.* 2nd ed. Minneapolis: Fortress Press, 2002.

———. *Theology of the Old Testament: Testimony, Dispute, Advocacy.* Minneapolis: Fortress Press, 1997.
Brueggemann, Walter, and Hans Walter Wolff. *The Vitality of Old Testament Traditions.* Atlanta: John Knox Press, 1975.
Butler, Trent C. *Joshua.* Word Biblical Commentary 7. Waco, Tex.: Word Books, 1983.
Calvin, John. *Commentaries on the Book of Joshua.* Translated by Henry Beveridge. Grand Rapids, Mich.: Eerdmans, 1949.
———. *Commentary on Joshua.* Available at http://www.ccel.org/ccel/calvin/calcom07 (last accessed January 2012).
Campbell, Antony F., and Mark A. O'Brien. *Unfolding the Deuteronomistic History: Origins, Upgrades, Present Text.* Minneapolis: Fortress Press, 2000.
Campbell, K. M. "Rahab's Covenant: A Short Note on Joshua 2:9–21." *Vetus Testamentum* 22 (1972): 243–44.
Childs, Brevard. *Biblical Theology of the Old and New Testaments: Theological Reflection on the Christian Bible.* Minneapolis: Fortress Press, 1992.
———. "The Etiological Tale Re-examined." *Vetus Testamentum* 24 (1974): 387–97.
———. "Study of the Formula, 'Until This Day.'" *Journal of Biblical Literature* 82 (1963): 279–92.
Cohen, C. "Rahab." In *Encyclopaedia Judaica,* vol. 17, 66–67. 2nd ed., edited by Michael Berenbaum and Frank Skolnik. 22 vols. Detroit: Macmillan Reference USA, 2007.
Collins, John. "The Zeal of Phinehas: The Bible and the Legitimation of Violence." *Journal of Biblical Literature* 122 (2003): 3–21.
Creach, Jerome F. D. *Joshua.* Interpretation. Louisville, Ky.: Westminster John Knox Press, 2003.
Cross, Frank Moore. *Canaanite Myth and Hebrew Epic: Essays in the History of the Religion of Israel.* Cambridge, Mass.: Harvard University Press, 1997.
———. "Response to Yair Zakovitch." In *Text and Tradition,* edited by Susan Niditch, 99–104.
———. "The Themes of the Book of Kings and the Structure of the Deuteronomistic History." In *Canaanite Myth and Hebrew Epic: Essays in the History of the Religion of Israel,* 274–89.
Cross, Frank Moore, and G. E. Wright. "The Boundary and Province Lists of the Kingdom of Judah." *Journal of Biblical Literature* 75 (1956): 202–26.
de Pury, Albert, Thomas Römer, and Jean-Daniel Macchi, eds. *Israel Constructs Its History: Deuteronomistic Historiography in Recent Research.* Journal for the Study of the Old Testament Supplement Series 306. Sheffield, England: Sheffield Academic Press, 2000.

Delsman, W. C., et al., eds. *Von Kanaan bis Kerala: Festschrift für Prof. Mag. Dr. J. P. M. van der Ploeg, O.P.* Kevelaer, Germany: Butzon and Bercker, 1982.

Driver, Samuel. *Introduction to the Literature of the Old Testament.* New York: Charles Scribner's Sons, 1916. Reprint, Whitefish, Mont.: Kessinger Publishing, 2005.

Earl, Douglas S. *Reading Joshua as Christian Scripture. Journal of Theological Interpretation* Supplement 2, edited by Murray Rae. Winona Lake, Ind.: Eisenbrauns, 2010.

Eissfeldt, Otto. *The Old Testament: An Introduction.* Translated by Peter R. Ackroyd from 3rd German ed. Oxford: Basil Blackwell, 1965.

Ellens, Deborah, Michael Floyd, Wonil Kim, and Marvin A. Sweeney, eds. *Reading the Hebrew Bible for a New Millennium: Form, Concept, and Theological Perspective.* Vol. 1, *Theological and Hermeneutical Studies.* Harrisburg, Pa.: Trinity Press International, 2000.

Fohrer, Georg. *Introduction to the Old Testament.* Translated by David E. Green. Nashville: Abingdon, 1968.

Frei, Hans. *The Eclipse of Biblical Narrative: A Study in Eighteenth and Nineteenth Century Hermeneutics.* New Haven: Yale University Press, 1974.

Geoghegan, Jeffrey C. *The Time, Place, and Purpose of the Deuteronomistic History: The Evidence of "Until This Day."* Brown Judaic Studies 347. Providence, R.I.: SBL, 2006.

Goldingay, John. "Justice and Salvation for Israel and Canaan." In *Reading the Hebrew Bible for a New Millennium,* edited by Deborah Ellens et al., 169–87.

Gottwald, Norman. "Religious Conversion and the Societal Origins of Ancient Israel." *Perspectives in Religious Studies* 15, no. 4 (1988): 49–65.

———. *The Tribes of [YHWH]: A Sociology of the Religion of Liberated Israel, 1250–1050 BCE.* Maryknoll, N.Y.: Orbis Press, 1979.

Gray, John. *Joshua, Judges and Ruth.* New Century Bible Commentary, edited by Ronald E. Clements and Matthew Black. Grand Rapids, Mich.: Eerdmans, 1986.

Greenspoon, Leonard. "The Book of Joshua, Part 1: Texts and Versions." *Currents in Biblical Research* 3 (2005): 229–61.

Gressmann, Hugo. *Die Schriften des Alten Testaments.* Göttingen: Vandenhoeck & Ruprecht, 1922.

Gunkel, Hermann. *Genesis.* Translated by Mark E. Biddle. Macon, Ga.: Mercer University Press, 1997.

Gunn, David M. "Joshua-Judges." In *The Literary Guide to the Bible,* edited by Robert Alter and Frank Kermode, 102–21. Cambridge, Mass.: Belknap Press, 1990.

Halpern, Baruch, and Jon D. Levenson, eds. *Traditions in Transformation: Turning Points in Biblical Faith.* Winona Lake, Ind.: Eisenbrauns, 1981.

Hamlin, E. John. *Inheriting the Land: A Commentary on the Book of Joshua*. International Theological Commentary. Grand Rapids, Mich.: Eerdmans, 1983.

Hawk, L. Daniel. "Conquest Reconfigured: Recasting Warfare in the Redaction of Joshua." In *Writing and Reading War*, edited by Brad E. Kelle and Frank Ritchel Ames, 145–60. Atlanta: SBL, 2008.

———. *Every Promise Fulfilled: Contesting Plots in Joshua*. Literary Currents in Biblical Interpretation. Louisville, Ky.: Westminster John Knox Press, 1991.

———. *Joshua*. Berit Olam: Studies in Hebrew Narrative and Poetry. Collegeville, Minn.: Liturgical Press, 2000.

Hoffman, Yair. "The Deuteronomistic Concept of the Ḥerem." *Zeitschrift für die alttestamentliche Wissenschaft* 111 (1999): 196–210.

Hoppe, Leslie. *Joshua, Judges with Excursus on Charismatic Leadership in Israel*. Old Testament Message 5. Collegeville, Minn.: Liturgical Press, 1982.

Kallai-Kleinmann, Z. "The Town Lists of Judah, Simeon, Benjamin and Dan." *Vetus Testamentum* 8 (1958): 134–60.

Kaminsky, Joel S. *Corporate Responsibility in the Hebrew Bible*. Journal for the Study of the Old Testament Supplement 196. Sheffield, England: Sheffield Academic Press, 1995.

———. *Yet I Loved Jacob: Reclaiming the Biblical Concept of Election*. Nashville: Abingdon, 2007.

Kaufmann, Yehezkel. *The Biblical Account of the Conquest of Canaan*. Translated and introduced by Moshe Greenberg. 2nd ed. Jerusalem: Magnes Press, 1985.

Kermode, Frank. *The Sense of an Ending: Studies in the Theory of Fiction*. London: Oxford, 1966.

Kloppenborg, John S. "Joshua 22: The Priestly Editing of an Ancient Tradition." *Biblica* 62 (1981): 347–71.

Knoppers, Gary. "There Was None Like Him: Incomparability in the Books of Kings." *Catholic Biblical Quarterly* 54, no. 3 (1992): 411–31.

Knoppers, Gary, and J. Gordon McConville, eds. *Reconsidering Israel and Judah: Recent Studies on the Deuteronomistic History*. Sources for Biblical and Theological Study 8. Winona Lake, Ind.: Eisenbrauns, 2000.

Kritzinger, J. P. L. "Rahab, illa meretrix." *Acta Patristica et Byzantina* 17 (2006): 22–36.

Lemaire, Andre. "Toward a Redactional History of the Book of Kings." In *Reconsidering Israel and Judah*, edited by Gary Knoppers and Gordon McConville, 449–61. Translated by S. W. Heldenbrand.

Lemche, Niels Peter. *The Canaanites and Their Land: The Tradition of the Canaanites*. Journal for the Study of the Old Testament Supplement Series

110. Edited by David J. A. Clines and Philip R. Davies. Sheffield, England: JSOT Press, 1991.

Levenson, Jon D. *Creation and the Persistence of Evil: The Jewish Drama of Divine Omnipotence*. Princeton, N.J.: Princeton University Press, 1988.

———. *The Death and Resurrection of the Beloved Son: The Transformation of Child Sacrifice in Judaism and Christianity*. New Haven: Yale University Press, 1993.

———. "From Temple to Synagogue: 1 Kings 8." In *Traditions in Transformation*, edited by Baruch and Jon D. Levenson, 143–66.

———. *The Hebrew Bible, the Old Testament, and Historical Criticism*. Louisville, Ky.: Westminster John Knox Press, 1993.

———. *Sinai and Zion: An Entry into the Jewish Bible*. San Francisco: HarperOne, 1987.

———. "Who Inserted the Book of the Torah?" *Harvard Theological Review* 68, no. 3–4 (1975): 203–33.

Lohfink, Norbert. "Auslegung deuteronomischer Texte, IV." *Bibel und Leben* 4 (1964): 247–56.

———. "Ḥaram." In *Theological Dictionary of the Old Testament*, edited by G. Johannes Botterweck, Helmer Ringgren, and Heinz-Josef Fabry, vol. 5, 180–99. Translated by David E. Green. Grand Rapids, Mich.: Eerdmans, 1995.

MacDonald, Nathan. *Deuteronomy and the Meaning of "Monotheism."* Forschungen zum alten Testament 2. Reihe 1. Tübingen: Mohr Siebeck, 2003.

Machinist, Peter. "Outsiders or Insiders: The Biblical View of Emergent Israel and Its Contexts." In *The Other in Jewish Thought and History: Constructions of Jewish Culture and Identity*, edited by Laurence J. Silberstein and Robert L. Cohn, 35–60. New York: New York University Press, 1994.

———. "The Question of Distinctiveness in Ancient Israel: An Essay." In *Ah, Assyria . . . Studies in Assyrian History and Ancient Near Eastern Historiography Presented to Hayim Tadmor*, edited by Mordechai Cogan and Israel Eph'al, 196–212. Jerusalem: Magnes, 1991.

McKenzie, Steven. "Deuteronomistic History." *The Anchor Bible Dictionary on CD-ROM*. 1994. Print ed.: David Noel Freedman, ed. *Anchor Bible Dictionary*. 6 vols. New York: Doubleday, 1992.

Milgrom, Jacob. "Religious Conversion and the Revolt Model for the Formation of Israel." *Journal of Biblical Literature* 101 (1982): 169–76.

Miller, Robert D., II. "Identifying Earliest Israel." *Bulletin of the American Schools of Oriental Research* 333 (Fall 2004): 55–68.

Mitchell, Gordon. *Together in the Land: A Reading of the Book of Joshua*. Journal for the Study of the Old Testament Supplement Series 134. Sheffield, England: JSOT Press, 1993.

Moberly, R. W. L. "Toward an Interpretation of the Shema." In *Theological Exegesis*, edited by Christopher Seitz and Kathryn Greene-McCreight, 124–44.

Nelson, Richard D. *The Double Redaction of the Deuteronomistic History*. Journal for the Study of the Old Testament Supplement Series 18. Sheffield, England: Sheffield University Press, 1981.

———. *Joshua: A Commentary*. Old Testament Library. Louisville, Ky.: Westminster John Knox Press, 1997.

———. "Josiah in the Book of Joshua." *Journal of Biblical Literature* 100 (1981): 531–40.

Niditch, Susan. *War in the Hebrew Bible: A Study in the Ethics of Violence*. New York: Oxford University Press, 1993.

———, ed. *Text and Tradition: The Hebrew Bible and Folklore*. The Society of Biblical Literature Semeia Studies. Atlanta: Scholars Press, 1990.

Noth, Martin. *Das Buch Josua*. Handbuch zum alten Testament, erste Reihe 7. Tübingen: Mohr Siebeck, 1938.

———. *The Deuteronomistic History*. 1943; Sheffield, England: University of Sheffield, 1981.

Organ, Barbara. "Pursuing Phinehas: A Synchronic Reading." *Catholic Biblical Quarterly* 63, no. 2 (2001): 203–18.

Pfeiffer, Robert H. *Introduction to the Old Testament*. New York/London: Harper & Brothers, 1941.

Polzin, Robert. *Moses and the Deuteronomist: A Literary Study of the Deuteronomistic History; Part One: Deuteronomy, Joshua, Judges*. New York: Seabury Press, 1980.

Provan, Iain W. *Hezekiah and the Books of Kings: A Contribution to the Debate about the Composition of the Deuteronomistic History*. Beihefte zur Zeitschrift für die alttestamentliche Wissenschaft 172. Berlin: Walter de Gruyter, 1988.

Rabinowitz, Louis Isaac, and David Max Eichhorn. "Proselytes." In *Encyclopaedia Judaica*, edited by Michael Berenbaum and Frank Skolnik, vol. 16, 587–94. 2nd ed. 22 vols. Detroit: Macmillan Reference USA, 2007.

Ricoeur, Paul. *Time and Narrative*. Vol. 1. Translated by K. McLaughlin and D. Pellauer. Chicago: University of Chicago, 1984.

Rofe, Alexander. "The Laws of Warfare in the Book of Deuteronomy: Their Origins, Intents and Positivity." *Journal for the Study of the Old Testament* 32 (1985): 23–44.

Roth, Wolfgang. "Deuteronomic Rest Theology: A Redaction-Critical Study." *Biblical Research* 21 (1976): 5–14.

Rowlett, Lori L. *Joshua and the Rhetoric of Violence: A New Historicist Analysis*. Journal for the Study of the Old Testament Supplement Series 226. Sheffield, England: Sheffield Academic Press, 1996.

Schwartz, Baruch. "Reexamining the Fate of the 'Canaanites' in the Torah Traditions." In *Sefer Moshe: The Moshe Weinfeld Jubilee Volume*, edited by Chaim Cohen, Avi Hurvitz, and Shalom M. Paul, 151–70. Winona Lake, Ind.: Eisenbrauns, 2004.

Seitz, Christopher, and Kathryn Greene-McCreight, eds. *Theological Exegesis: Essays in Honor of Brevard Childs*. Grand Rapids, Mich.: Eerdmans, 1999.

Smend, Rudolf. "Die Gesetz und die Völker: Ein Beitrag zur deuteronomistischen Redaktionsgeschichte." In *Probleme biblischer Theologie*, edited by Hans Walter Wolff, 494–509.

Snaith, N. H. "The Altar at Gilgal: Joshua XXII 23–29." *Vetus Testamentum* 28 (1978): 330–35.

Soggin, J. Alberto. *Joshua: A Commentary*. Old Testament Library. London: SCM Press, 1972.

Spina, Frank A. *The Faith of the Outsider: Exclusion and Inclusion in the Biblical Story*. Grand Rapids, Mich.: Eerdmans, 2005.

Stander, H. F. "The Greek Church Fathers and Rahab." *Acta Patristica et Byzantina* 17 (2006): 37–49.

Stern, Philip D. *The Biblical Ḥerem: A Window on Israel's Religious Experience*. Brown Judaic Studies 211. Atlanta: Scholars Press, 1991.

Sternberg, Meir. *The Poetics of Biblical Narrative: Ideological Literature and the Drama of Reading*. Bloomington: Indiana University Press, 1987.

Taylor, Charles. *A Secular Age*. Cambridge, Mass.: Belknap Press, 2007.

Teigen, Ragnar C. "Joshua's Total Conquest of Canaan: A Theological Rationale." *Consensus* 11, no. 4 (1985): 23–30.

Tov, Emmanuel. *The Greek and Hebrew Bible: Collected Essays on the Septuagint*. Supplements to *Vetus Testamentum* 72. Leiden: Brill, 1999.

———. "The Growth of the Book of Joshua." In *The Greek and Hebrew Bible*, 385–96.

———. "Some Sequence Differences between the Masoretic Text and the Septuagint and Their Ramifications for Literary Criticism." In *The Greek and Hebrew Bible*, 411–18.

van der Toorn, Karel. "Female Prostitution in Payment of Vows in Ancient Israel." *Journal of Biblical Literature* 108 (1989): 193–205.

von Rad, Gerhard. "The Deuteronomistic Theology of History in the Books of Kings." In *Studies in Deuteronomy*, 74–91.

———. *Deuteronomy: A Commentary*. Old Testament Library. Louisville, Ky.: Westminster John Knox Press, 1996.

———. "The Form-Critical Problem of the Hexateuch." In *The Problem of the Hexateuch and Other Essays*, 1–78.

———. *The Problem of the Hexateuch and Other Essays*. Translated by E. W. Trueman Dicken. Edinburgh/London: Oliver & Boyd, 1966.

———. "The Promised Land and YHWH's Land in the Hexateuch." In *The Problem of the Hexateuch and Other Essays*, 79–93.

———. *Studies in Deuteronomy*. Translated by D. Stalker. Chicago: Henry Regnery, 1953.

———. "There Remains Still a Rest for the People of God: An Investigation of a Biblical Conception." In *The Problem of the Hexateuch and Other Essays*, 94–102.

Weinfeld, Moshe. *Deuteronomy and the Deuteronomic School*. Winona Lake, Ind.: Eisenbrauns, 1992.

———. *The Promise of the Land: The Inheritance of the Land of Canaan by the Israelites*. Berkeley: University of California Press, 1993.

Weippert, Helga. "Die 'deuteronomistischen' Beurteilungen der Könige von Israel und Juda und das Problem der Redaktion der Königsbücher." *Biblica* 53 (1972): 301–39.

Wolff, Hans Walter. "Das Kerygma des deuteronomistischen Geschichtswerks." *Zeitschrift für die alttestamentliche Wissenschaft* 73 (1961): 171–86.

———, ed. *Probleme biblischer Theologie: Gerhard von Rad zum 70. Geburtstag*. Munich: Kaiser Verlag, 1971.

Wood, Bryant. "Did the Israelites Conquer Jericho? A New Look at the Archaeological Evidence." *Biblical Archaeology Review* 16, no. 2 (1990): 44–58

Woudstra, Marten H. *The Book of Joshua*. New International Commentary on the Old Testament. Grand Rapids, Mich.: Eerdmans, 1981.

Wright, G. E. "The Literary and Historical Problem of Joshua 10 and Judges 1." *Journal of Near Eastern Studies* 5 (1946): 105–14.

Younger, K. Lawson, Jr. *Ancient Conquest Accounts: A Study in Ancient Near Eastern and Biblical History Writing*. Journal for the Study of the Old Testament Supplement Series 98. Sheffield, England: JSOT Press, 1990.

Zakovitch, Yair. "Humor and Theology or the Successful Failure of Israelite Intelligence: A Literary-Folkloric Approach to Joshua 2." In *Text and Tradition*, edited by Susan Niditch, 73–98.

Zimmerli, Walter. "The 'Land' in the Pre-Exilic and Early Post-Exilic Prophets." In *Understanding the Word: Essays in Honor of Bernhard W. Anderson*, edited by James T. Butler, Edgar W. Conrad, and Ben C. Ollenburger, 247–62. Journal for the Study of the Old Testament Supplement Series 37. Sheffield, England: JSOT Press, 1985.

Index

Achan
  and the *ḥerem,* 36, 37, 55, 57, 135n5, 145n2, 152n69
  literary function of, 12, 23, 28, 46, 145n4
  vs. Rahab, 37, 138n1
  See also *ḥerem,* violation by Achan; sin, of Achan

Ai
  first Israelite attempt to conquer, 47, 143n65, 153n73
  second Israelite attempt to conquer, 54–55

altar, Transjordanian
  legitimacy of, 22–23, 53–54, 89–90, 127, 137n28
  literary function of, 12, 22–23, 79–80, 82, 145n4
  meaning of, 79–80, 83, 85–86, 89–90, 91, 92, 120, 153n76, 154n77, 156n99

altars
  absence of Canaanite, 153n74
  in Joshua, 55, 153n74

  Josiah's destruction of, 71, 81
  as *tabnît,* 90–91, 156n101, 156n103

ancestors. *See* promise, to the ancestors

archaeology, 2

Canaanites
  conversion of (*see* conversion to Israel)
  corvée labor, 109, 110, 113, 160n34
  literary role, 8, 25–27, 33, 35, 37, 44, 47, 51, 61, 66, 71, 73–75, 152n67
  remaining in the land, 13, 22–23, 25–27, 28–29, 35–36, 43, 57, 59, 61, 65, 66, 69–70, 72, 98, 101, 105, 106, 108, 109–11, 112–14, 115, 118, 122, 123, 126–27, 128, 148n28, 151n55, 159n29, 160n32, 160nn34–35

Childs, Brevard, 3, 7, 136n15, 137n21

Cisjordanian tribes, 78, 85–86, 89, 91, 104, 116, 127, 153n75, 155n90, 156n99

173

INDEX

confession
  Achan's (of guilt), 144n75
  the Gibeonites' (of faith in YHWH), 60, 147n14
  Rahab's (of faith in YHWH), 32–35, 37–38, 40–41, 42, 43–44
conquest, 1, 5, 6, 8, 20–21, 62, 64, 65, 70, 72, 78, 95–96, 101–2, 103, 105, 112, 116, 118, 121, 122, 123, 134n11, 158n12, 161n48
conversion to Israel, 38–39, 41–43
  definition of, 142n51, 142n56
  and ethnic identity, 42–43, 59, 141n40
  and Rahab's confession, 40–41, 120
covenant, 33–34
  between Israel and Rahab, 26–27, 28, 35–36, 37–38, 43, 139n11, 141n38
  between Israel and the Gibeonites, 53, 56–57, 147n12
  between YHWH and Israel, 12, 14–16, 21, 23, 45–46, 49–50, 51, 55, 57, 58–59, 92, 114, 123, 131, 137n26, 144n74, 145n6, 146n11, 158n11, 161n39

Deuteronomistic historian (Dtr), 5–6, 7–9, 15, 18–19, 21–23, 25, 28, 64–65, 73–74, 75, 80, 82, 89–90, 91, 130, 137n29, 140n28, 140n33, 141n38, 145n1, 149n48, 151n56, 154nn78–79, 154n82, 156n96, 161n41, 162n49, 162n52
Deuteronomistic History (DtrH), 1–2, 4–6, 9–10, 24, 29, 32, 33, 35–36, 41, 64–70, 71–73, 81, 99, 118, 119, 133n7, 135n10, 148n27, 148n30, 150n52, 154n84, 156n101, 160nn33–34, 161nn42–43, 161n48, 162n49, 162n52
Deuteronomy, 9, 18–19, 22–23, 25, 32–33, 35–37, 41, 42, 43–44, 57, 61, 65, 66–70, 71–74, 75–76, 127, 128, 134n18, 135n5, 137nn28–29, 138n10, 139n16, 140n28, 143n69, 144n73, 145n6, 146n11, 148n24, 148n26, 148n28, 148n34, 148n39, 149n41, 149n46, 150nn50–51, 151n55, 152nn67–68, 153n74

election, 33, 39–40, 54, 91, 98–99, 113–14, 144n76

faithfulness
  of Israel to YHWH, 8–9, 12–14, 23, 24, 43, 45–46, 50, 51, 53–54, 58–59, 77, 78, 82, 83–86, 89, 90, 93, 110, 115, 126–27
  of Joshua to YHWH, 48–49, 103–4, 117, 135n3, 137n24
  of Rahab to Israel and YHWH, 125
  of YHWH to Israel, 34, 49–50, 51, 52, 59, 97–98, 104, 107, 125, 126, 146n11

Gibeonites, 6–7, 12, 22, 53, 54, 56–61, 87, 129
  treaty with Israel, 56–57, 58–59, 93, 126–27, 137n25, 143n59, 146n11, 147n12, 152n69, 153n73
  See also confession, the Gibeonites'; ḥerem, exemption from, Gibeonites
Gunn, David, 10

INDEX

Hawk, L. Daniel, 10, 28–29, 102–3, 120–21, 129, 138n9, 140n22, 141n35, 143n60, 144n73, 145n6, 146nn7–8, 152n69, 153n71, 153n75, 155nn90–92, 156nn98–99, 159n22, 162n53
ḥerem, 13, 36, 42, 56, 135n5, 136n16, 138n10, 148nn23–24, 149n40, 152n66
  excursus on, 61–77
  exemption from
  —Gibeonites, 47, 57–58, 59, 60–61, 77–78, 93, 101, 126–27, 143n59, 146n7, 146n11, 152n69
  —Rahab, 27, 29, 32, 35, 37, 43–44, 47, 60
  historical background, 24, 62–64, 72, 76–77, 148nn23–24, 149n47, 151n62
  Israel as, 49–50, 69, 70–76, 144n76, 153n74
  literary development of, 64–65, 65–70, 73–74, 140n33, 148n27, 148n30, 148n39, 149n43, 149n45, 149n47, 150nn49–51, 151nn55–56, 151n62
  as metaphor, 62, 66–67, 69–71, 73–74, 148n39
  violation by Achan, 12, 13, 22, 23, 25–26, 36–37, 45–46, 51, 57–58, 126, 145n2
hermeneutics, 63
  hermeneutical clues, 19, 24
  hermeneutical dilemma, 79–80, 148n28
  hermeneutical key, 12, 17, 24, 125, 129–30, 136n15
  See also Joshua 24:31; text, as hermeneutical medium
humor. See Joshua, book of, humor in

inheritance. See land, as inheritance
irony. See Joshua, book of, irony in

Joshua, book of
  canonical context of, 24, 35, 135n10, 136n15, 137n21
  etiological readings of, 5–6, 7, 154n82
  humor in, 27–28, 32, 138n7, 140n22
  irony in, 11, 55–56, 59–60, 78, 79, 96, 117, 153n76
  literary readings of, 9–10, 15, 16, 80, 134n17, 140n22, 148n39, 150n51, 151n56, 155n90, 160n36
  tensions in, 9–10, 11–12, 14, 17–19, 20, 23–24, 25, 26–27, 29, 43, 45–46, 51–52, 57, 93, 96, 97–99, 100–101, 103, 108, 114–15, 137n29, 138n10, 161n48
Joshua, person
  complaint of, 47–49, 51, 143n69, 146n7
  days of, 11–12, 19, 47, 54, 109, 125, 129, 135n7
  leadership of, 12, 14, 15, 20, 23, 102–3, 114–15, 116, 130
Joshua 24:31, 11–12, 14, 16, 17, 23–24, 125, 145n4. See also hermeneutics, hermeneutical key

Kaminsky, Joel, 39–40, 144n76

land
  as gift, 62, 98–99, 100, 110, 117, 119, 128, 137n24, 161n46
  as inheritance, 7, 20–21, 65, 74, 79, 95–96, 104, 110, 118, 119–20

land (*cont.*)
    settlement of, 2–3, 8, 25, 78, 97–99, 105, 111–12, 116
    taking of, 8–9, 20, 23–24, 73, 78, 95–99, 101–2, 103, 104–6, 116–17, 120, 128, 158n12
Law, 8–9, 18, 20–23, 24, 26–27, 28–29, 36, 44–45, 54–56, 93, 96–97, 117, 129, 138n10, 140n29
    book of the, 8–9, 20–23, 35, 55, 56, 72–73, 116–17, 126–27, 137n26, 137n29, 145n1, 145n3, 150n53
    Torah, 8–9, 21–22, 35, 72–73, 96–97, 100–101, 126–27, 130–31, 137n29, 145n1, 154n84
laws, 12, 31, 34–37, 39, 43, 56, 72, 73, 126, 139n16
Levenson, Jon, 72–73, 74, 137n29, 140n28, 150n53, 161n39, 161n47

MacDonald, Nathan, 32–33, 65–67, 70–71, 140n24, 148n28, 148n34, 148n39, 149nn40–41, 151n55, 151n62, 152n67
Mitchell, Gordon, 10, 47, 103, 121, 135n5, 135n7, 135n10, 136n16, 138n1, 141n34, 142n45, 143n69, 144n74, 147n12, 147n14
Moberly, Walter, 65, 66, 67, 70, 71, 148n34, 149nn40–41
Moses, 33, 48, 55–56, 69–70, 84–85, 101, 103, 104, 106–7, 116–17, 135n3, 137n24, 144n73, 146n11, 159n22

Nelson, Richard, 9–10, 40, 49, 71, 129, 149n48, 150n50, 159n23
Noth, Martin, 1–2, 5–6

oath
    to the ancestors, 117 (*see also* promise, to the ancestors)
    to the Gibeonites, 56–59, 93, 126–27, 152n69
    to Rahab, 12, 22, 26–27, 28–29, 34–38, 43–44, 77, 138n10, 139nn11–12, 141n35, 143n60
obedience. *See under* faithfulness

Phinehas, 81–83, 87–88, 90–92, 155n95, 156nn96–97
Polzin, Robert, 9, 20, 22, 36, 96, 97, 117, 121, 129
priestly, 82–83, 88–89, 91, 154n78, 154n84, 156n96
promise (YHWH's), 10, 13, 21, 25, 33–34, 47–49, 50, 51, 64, 75, 79, 96–98, 99, 100–101, 105, 106, 109, 110, 112–14, 115–18, 119, 122–23, 126, 146n11, 152n68, 153n71, 155n89, 157n6, 159n23, 160n35
    to the ancestors, 75, 78–79, 100, 115–16, 117, 146n11, 155n89

Rahab, 26–41
    as ally, 26–29, 51–52
    confession of, 32–34, 40–43
    exemption from the *ḥerem*, 36, 37–41
    literary function of, 6, 25–32, 37–38, 43, 45
    oath to (*see* oath, to Rahab)
    survival of, 37
redaction, 17, 19, 137n21
repentance, 12, 17, 18, 26, 27, 44–46, 54, 111

sacrifice, 22–23, 137n28, 147n15

sin
- corporate, 58, 87, 126, 144n75
- of Achan, 13, 22, 44–45, 46, 50, 54, 55, 58, 83–84
- —corporate responsibility and, 44–46, 50, 51, 109, 126, 144nn75–76
- of Israel, 44–46, 54, 57–58, 59, 74–75
- personal/individual, 45, 46
- *See also* Achan

spies, 25–30, 32, 34–37, 38, 43–44, 138n3

subversion, 8, 25, 44, 52, 120

text (biblical)
- as basis for interpretation, 3–4
- and canonical context, 24, 35
- in conversation with the reader, 3, 120–23, 136n19
- as hermeneutical medium, 36, 97, 162n49
- as self-contained entity, 4, 5
- as source vs. witness 3, 81, 133n6
- as story, 3–4, 6, 7, 8, 18, 19, 23, 26–28, 29, 38, 43–44, 45, 77, 78, 80–82, 91, 98, 100
- theological interpretation of, 3, 7, 11–12, 18–19, 73, 99–101, 151n56, 151n63

Torah. *See* Law

"to this day," 7, 55, 110, 114

Transjordanian tribes, 22, 51, 63, 78–92

treaty, 12, 13, 56–61, 77, 126–27, 137n25, 143n59, 146n11

von Rad, Gerhard, 1, 150n50, 161n42

worship, 79, 80, 82, 83, 86, 89, 90–91, 127–28

YHWH
- ongoing work of, 7, 79, 98–99, 104, 105, 107, 119, 128
- *See also* faithfulness, of YHWH to Israel

Rachel M. Billings

is an independent scholar in Holland, Michigan.

www.ingramcontent.com/pod-product-compliance
Lightning Source LLC
Chambersburg PA
CBHW061448300426
44114CB00014B/1886